S - 5/4/22
F - 7/4/22

CANTONA
THE RED AND THE BLACK

CANTONA

THE RED AND THE BLACK

Ian Ridley

VICTOR GOLLANCZ

LONDON

First published in Great Britain 1995
by Victor Gollancz
An imprint of the Cassell Group
Wellington House, 125 Strand, London WC2R OBB

A catalogue record for this book is
available from the British Library.

ISBN 0 575 06130 8

Set in Linotron Bembo by
Rowland Phototypesetting Ltd
Bury St Edmunds, Suffolk

Printed in Great Britain by
Mackays of Chatham plc, Chatham, Kent

Contents

Acknowledgements

Firstly I thank Eric Cantona for being, well, Eric Cantona, and so worth writing about, no matter what one's opinion of him. Speaking of which, everyone seems to have one, which is useful when you are approaching a biography of him. I am very grateful to those who were willing, and brave enough, to contribute theirs publicly. In France Gérard Houllier, Henri Émile, Erik Bielderman and Jean-Philippe Leclaire were especially helpful; in England Lee Chapman, Chris Waddle and David Meek. Howard Wilkinson and Alex Ferguson felt able to offer only limited help but I thank them for that nevertheless.

Beyond people who have known the subject well, I have consulted many books, magazines and videos in an attempt to get as full a picture as possible. Naturally, I began with the autobiography, *Cantona – My Story*. I have also drawn from Howard Wilkinson's autobiography *Managing to Succeed*, Mark Hughes's *Hughesie*, Lee Chapman's *More than a Match* and Jim White's semi-autobiographical *Are You Watching, Liverpool?* Two videos, *Eric the King*, and *Ooh-aah, Cantona* have also been useful. I have further drawn from most sections of the English press and from *L'Équipe*, *L'Équipe* magazine, *Globe Hebdo*, *Le Sport* and *France Football* across the Channel. All are given due recognition in the text where appropriate.

Many journalists shared their time, insight and expertise, notably John Ley, who helped with early research, Paul Newman, Henry Winter, Patrick Barclay, Joe Lovejoy, Phil Shaw,

Colin Malam, David Walker, Peter Fitton and Ken Lawrence. I would also like to thank my former sports editors at the *Guardian* and *Daily Telegraph*, John Samuel and David Welch, for their parts in my career thus far, and the current, marvellous crew with whom I work at the *Independent on Sunday*: the sports editor Simon Kelner, his deputy Neil Morton and assistant Ben Clissitt.

Simon, experienced with my copy, offered counselling to Richard Wigmore and Ian Preece at Victor Gollancz before they set about the manuscript but they were more than capable, the one excellent broad brush, the other thorough pointilliste. I am grateful to them, and my literary agent John Pawsey, for their vital roles in this book's conception and execution.

As I have lived it, my wife Jo and children Alexandra and Jack have missed out on much and put up with more; I am more grateful than they can know for their support, tolerance and encouragement. Heartfelt gratitude, too, to Jimmy Mulville, a great friend and supplier of the title; Bruce Lloyd, an inspirational confidant; and finally Bill W, without whom it would not have been possible.

1 Cantona Protagoniste

You've got a very heavy reputation,
But no one knows about your low life,
I know a way to find a situation
And hold a candle to your high-life disguise.
David Bowie, 'Criminal World'

There is only one starting point with Eric Cantona: Selhurst Park, home of Crystal Palace Football Club, at 8.57 p.m. on 25 January, 1995. There is only one verdict on what Cantona did that night, the third anniversary of his arrival in England. When he launched himself feet-first over a barrier into a Palace fan, whom he then punched as retaliation for calling him a French motherfucker, it was, quite simply, wrong. To condemn the act should not be to condemn the man, however.

In the shocked aftermath of that night there were calls for Cantona to be kicked out of the game for ever. It was the reaction to something so bizarre, so astonishing. 'I'd cut his balls off,' was the less-than-cogent response on television of the former Nottingham Forest manager Brian Clough. The *Sun* called for him to be drummed out of the game. From the left of the quoting party came this from Richard Kurt, author of the book *United We Stand*, to Jim White in the *Independent* magazine: 'There's something about Cantona which symbolizes what the hard-core United fan feels about themselves. Like him, we're picked on and hated because we reckon we are the best. What he was saying with that kick was what we want to say: "You cannot say that sort of thing to us and get away with it. We are United; respect us." At the time, there was a lot of talk about not condoning what he did, but I reckon at root we think it was a fantastic thing to do.' The *Guardian* headed a piece 'Why Eric was right to take a leap in the dark.'

It illustrated how polarized were the reactions to Cantona; hate him or love him. He himself would be pleased that he never inspired indifference. Readers of the football magazine *Four Four Two* voted it the best moment of the season and named him second in the 'cult hero' category behind Jürgen Klinsmann, even though he missed half the season. It was an image that Cantona played on. In an advertisement for his sponsors, the sportswear company Nike, whose strategy is based on performers with edge, he said: 'I have been punished for striking a goalkeeper. For spitting at supporters. For throwing my shirt at a referee. For calling my manager a bag of shit. I called those who judged me a bunch of idiots. I thought I might have trouble finding a sponsor.'

Then came the jokes: 'Eric's signing for Rangers – Power Rangers'; and 'He's very temperamental – fifty per cent temper and fifty per cent mental.' It was funny, too, when the *Observer*'s TV page carried a listing saying '9.50: Natural Born Killers Special: Eric Cantona.' 'He's lost *les marbles*,' said Gary Lineker on BBC television. In reality, though, it was a serious, sorry business. Naturally he had to be punished, and appropriately. There was a lot of talk of role models for kids being bandied about. But what kind of role models would adults be if forgiveness was not among their attributes?

With one bound, Cantona leapt from gifted-but-difficult footballer to public debate. The episode had followed the fifth sending off in his twenty-six months with Manchester United. The night after it happened I was dining in a hotel in Norfolk, a different, tranquil world from the cityscape clamour of English football, when the peace of the room was disturbed by an elderly tweed-suited gentleman. 'What's this Cantona fellow been and done now?' he asked, in a voice reminiscent of a 1950's BBC announcer. His prim wife told him not to be so silly, that there were far more important things to be talking about.

Actually, for a while there weren't. The following day, both BBC and ITN lunchtime news bulletins led on Manchester United's response to the act of their turbulent player – a ban until the end of the season and a fine of two weeks' wages. The story was placed ahead of the fiftieth anniversary remembrance service at Auschwitz. Winter turned to spring with *l'Affaire Cantona* still high on the agenda of both news and sports desks, and the ban was extended until 30 September by the Football Association, who also imposed a further fine of £10,000. Cantona was then found guilty of common assault at Croydon Magistrates Court and sentenced to two weeks' imprisonment, reduced on appeal to 120 hours of community service. The Italian club Internazionale of Milan sought to sign him. Should he stay or should he go? Finally, bravely, he decided to face what would surely be the cacophonous music.

Cantona brought out the amateur psychologist in all of us. What was beating in the breast tattooed with an Indian chief in full headdress? What was going on under that spiky, often dishevelled hair? The trademark turned-up collar evoked some worldly-wise movie star – Jack Nicholson in *Chinatown*, perhaps – embroiled in a me-against-the-world plot. The hauteur he brought to the press conference that followed the disciplinary and judicial trials, gave the impression of disdain for any who sat in judgement. '*Je ne regrette rien,*' his eyes said. 'Don't mess with me' might just as well have been written on his forehead.

The mystique was enhanced by the rarity of his interviews. This was due to poor English, he claimed, though those who have known him say he understands almost everything and can speak more than he lets on. His assertion after his court appeal that: 'When the seagulls follow the trawler, it is because they think that sardines will be thrown,' only fanned the flames of fascination. Pretentious, moi? It reminded you of Chance the gardener, played by Peter Sellers, in the film *Being There*. 'If I'd said that,' said a former colleague of Cantona's at Leeds, Gordon Strachan, 'I would just have been called a drunken Scotsman.' Still, many hung on to his every word, no matter how banal, as some pearl of wisdom. This observer was duly hooked. The temptation became to change the title of this book to 'Of Gauls and Gulls', or perhaps just simply 'Norman wisdom'.

Whimsy apart, *The Red and the Black* is intended to illustrate the dominant shades of Eric Cantona: the fiery and the dark. It is probably no coincidence that Manchester United were clad in black that night at Selhurst Park, nor that their first-choice colour is a vivid red. There are other colours and it's appropriate, if not symbolic, that United, with whom Cantona has enjoyed the mightiest, meatiest moments of his volatile career, play in more than most. There is, too, blue, and green and yellow.

Old Trafford has entered English football's folklore as the Theatre of Dreams. In two glorious seasons before the nightmare, Cantona was its Sandman, inducing the sweetest of reveries. United took the domestic game to a new plane with a pace and panache that had the hairs on your neck standing up in defiance of the all-seater ground regulations. In Alex Ferguson, an emotional Scot with a temper to match Cantona's, the Frenchman had at last found a club manager whose value of his worth coincided with his own. Cantona's touch, vision and balance brought the team the element of fantasy it was missing. His goals were more tangible reality. To the power came the glory. United, after the signing of Cantona from Leeds in November 1992, won the new Premier League's inaugural title that season: the grail Old Trafford had been desperately seeking for twenty-six years since Sir Matt Busby's team of George Best, Bobby Charlton and Denis Law had thrilled similarly. For good measure, Cantona inspired United to only the fourth Double – the classic league and FA Cup one-two – this century. He was named by his fellow professionals as the Footballer of the Year in 1994, the first foreign recipient of the award. 'Mon genius,' Ferguson called him.

The appeal went beyond the physical, beyond any footballing ability. I had seen him play for Leeds United but had not been especially impressed, though the cult following he attracted amongst the Elland Road fancy suggested something different.

When I saw him drive in a 25-yard shot for Manchester United against Arsenal, it confirmed his exciting capabilities as a player. Off the field the charisma became apparent. I saw him besieged by news crews at Barcelona airport before a European Cup tie he was not even playing in. I also saw, on the flight home, a stewardess gazing at his backside. 'He is quite good looking; not madly so,' one woman told me. 'But he is attractive. Very sexy.'

He became 'Eric the King' to Old Trafford's worshippers, assuming the title of Denis Law, who said that he could not think of a better person to whom it should go. At one United function, everyone stood to applaud him as he entered the room. 'I'd never seen that, not even with George Best,' said the former United player Paddy Crerand. Many fans wore replica No. 7 shirts not with 'Cantona' on them but 'God' or 'Dieu'. 'Ooh-aah, Cantona' they chanted at the Marseillais to the Marseillaise, the French national anthem.

There was, on top, an intellectual attraction in a man who transcended the stereotype of an English footballer as a steak-and-chips-chewing, BMW-driving, mock Tudor home-dwelling, lager-drinking, snooker-playing male bimbo. Cantona's interests were hunting, poetry – particularly the tempestuous Arthur Rimbaud – and art. 'I think the rest of us are painting by numbers,' said his former Manchester United team-mate Mark Hughes. Cantona and his wife Isabelle, not some buxom blonde trophy missus but a petite teacher of English at Leeds University, preferred modest suburban semis and functional cars. The writer Ian Hamilton had described devotees of Paul Gascoigne as 'Gazza agonistes'; Eric's fans were loyal to Cantona protagoniste. The abundant grey squirrels of the game exist in the leafy lanes; the rarer red squirrels, more dangerous, more beautiful, live on the edge of town. Cantona was both extraordinary and ordinary. 'That is Eric. I am a star, but I am a simple person,' says Erik Bielderman, a football writer with the French sports newspaper *L'Équipe*, who is as close to him as any journalist has ever been allowed to get. 'I live nearby you, but I am not you.'

The career has certainly been extraordinary. In France, Eric Cantona played for six different clubs – Auxerre, Martigues,

Marseille, Bordeaux, Montpellier and Nîmes – with controversy courting him at every stop: a team-mate punched here, a French manager insulted there; here a shirt thrown, there an absence, everywhere a walk-out. Michel Platini, formerly his manager with the French national team and probably the nation's greatest ever player, persuaded him that his heart and legs were made for England. His durable 6ft 1in, 12st 10lb frame was certainly right for the hurly-burly of the Premier League, while his nimble feet were to add something new. He endured a week's trial with Sheffield Wednesday but would not countenance another. Then a honeymoon of wild abandon with Leeds United – he told the fans after the title had been won: 'Why I love you, I don't know why, but I love you,' – ended with acrimonious divorce. 'Eric likes to do what he likes, when he likes, then fuck off. We'd all like a bit of that,' said a disillusioned Leeds manager Howard Wilkinson.

Finally he found *le club juste, au moment juste*. There was swiftly, breathtakingly, evidence of why he had somehow remained in demand despite all the problems, hitherto misdemeanours rather than felonies; a chemistry that suited the charisma. *Sans Cantona*, Manchester United were stripped of both elements and both trophies. They were suddenly second best in league and Cup; as it is given, so shall it be taken away. With him they had a *je ne sais quoi*, without him sometimes a *je ne sais pas*. A member of the disciplinary committee that once banned Cantona for two months in France said: 'You cannot be judged like any other player. Behind you there is a trail of the smell of sulphur.' Now the volcano had erupted.

It had been bubbling for some time, even through the good times. Amid the shock of Selhurst, one person within the game who had been connected with Cantona told me he saw it as 'an inevitable conclusion'. Herewith the evidence. In football magazines, players are asked for their worst and best moments in the game. Normally it takes up a few lines. With Cantona, it would take up a few issues. A top 10 might read something like:

WORST

1. Selhurst Park (not to mention the subsequent FA disciplinary hearing and two court appearances).

2. Screening a repeat for an ITN film crew in Guadeloupe.

3. Stamping on the stomach of Swindon's John Moncur.

4. Recklessly tackling from behind Norwich's Jeremy Goss, then, in the same match, kicking out at John Polston.

5. Punching his Auxerre team-mate Bruno Martini.

6. Throwing his boots in the face of his Montpellier colleague Jean-Claude Lemoult.

7. Describing the then manager of France, Henri Michel, as being 'not far' from '*un sac à merde*' – a shitbag – then being banned from the national team for a year.

8. Throwing his Marseille shirt to the ground during a match.

9. A sending off, and subsequent four-match ban, in Istanbul against Galatasaray.

10. Throwing the ball at a referee when playing for Nîmes, then announcing his retirement after being suspended for two months.

BEST

1. Winning the title (twice) with Manchester United.

2. Winning the title with Leeds United.

3. Winning the FA Cup with Manchester United.

4. Winning the French Cup with Montpellier.

5. Helping the French Under-21 team to the European Championship.

6. Scoring twice in a 4–2 win for France against Sweden.

7. A virtuoso solo goal for Leeds against Chelsea.

8. A chipped goal for Manchester United against Southampton.

9. A volleyed goal for Manchester United against Wimbledon.

10. An astonishing backheeled crossfield pass for a colleague to score for France's Under-21 side.

It is not so much a rollercoaster ride of a career as Space Mountain. And through it all, at the heart of it, and the man, are a series of contradictions which Erik Bielderman hinted at. 'There are two Eric Cantonas,' Michel Platini has said. 'The man himself and the man who talks.' 'I can contradict myself from one day to the next,' said Cantona himself in an interview with the French magazine *Globe Hebdo*. 'That's my prerogative. Contradiction goes hand in hand with sincerity.'

The word genius is overused in football but perhaps it does apply to Cantona. The Concise Oxford English dictionary defines it as: 'Two opposed spirits or angels working for person's salvation or damnation, also, person who powerfully influences one for good or ill; person having exalted intellectual power, instinctive and extraordinary, imaginative, creative or inventive capacity.'

The heroes he has listed reveal the dichotomies. A poster of the kung-fu king Bruce Lee stared down at him from his bedroom wall as a child. The Dutch master Johan Cruyff was also a boyhood footballing idol. Later, from French literature, there would be the poet Charles Pierre Baudelaire and the novelist-philosopher Antoine de St-Exupéry, as well as Arthur Rimbaud; from the cinema, Marlon Brando and Mickey Rourke; from painting – given to him, like football, by his father – Chagall and Miro; from music, David Bowie and Jim Morrison of The Doors. '[Morrison] always confirmed me in the feeling that I have always had of being free, tied to nothing except the great dream of life,' Cantona said in his somewhat cursory autobiography – published before the start of the momentous 1994–95 season and thus missing something or other – actually written by a French radio journalist Pierre-Louis Basse and titled *Un Rêve Modeste et Fou (A*

Simple, Mad Dream) in France but, more prosaically, *My Story* in England.

The idols say much. Rimbaud was a tortured young genius, who appropriately wrote a collection entitled *A Season in Hell*. He burned out young, dying in Cantona's home city of Marseille. He wrote of beauty, but also of ugliness. Lee also died young, as did Morrison, of the drugs that Cantona has always abhorred. Brando was the eponymous hero of *The Wild One*; Bowie wrote 'Rebel, Rebel' and 'Heroes'.

Cantona clearly sees himself as an artist and it is not fanciful. 'In every society . . . there are extraordinary men and women who, for a variety of reasons, stand outside the social consensus, shatter the norms and challenge the status quo,' wrote the American author Sam Keen in *Fire in the Belly*. 'These iconoclasts – prophets, rebels, revolutionaries, reformers, shamans, visionaries, mystics, artists, madmen, geniuses, schizophrenics – trouble the waters and disturb the majority but bring new creative energies into a society. As pathfinders of new ways of being and seeing, they pay a high personal price. They are often painfully self-conscious and lonely, and are both stranger and stronger than average folk.' In researching this book, talking to people who have known Cantona well, all those things emerged despite the lofty, don't-care attitude that he may seem to project.

What emerged, too, was Cantona's own sense of justice, mis-guided as it has often looked. In every episode in France, said Henri Émile, assistant coach of the French national side and a man who encouraged him as a junior player in Marseille, Cantona was reacting to a perceived injustice and passing his own sentence. It is a common thread, too, in England. It cannot be to condone. Only to seek to understand.

Cantona's bloodless Palace coup came at a particularly difficult time for the game. English football had begun the season so brightly with new stadiums completed and other stars of the Cantona calibre, notably the German Jürgen Klinsmann, having been attracted to the Premiership. Manchester United, with Cantona pulling the rope, had dragged the English game to a stage where it was adding finesse to the energy that had been its saving lack of grace. Newcastle United and Nottingham Forest were on the coat tails of the richer clubs, seeking to play progressive football.

But summer turned to autumn and optimism to cynicism. The Southampton and former Liverpool goalkeeper Bruce Grobbelaar was accused by the *Sun* of taking bribes, the Arsenal player Paul Merson accepted, very publicly, his alcoholism and gambling addiction, while his club manager George Graham was found to have received more than £400,000 as 'an unsolicited gift' from an agent who brokered the transfers to his club of two Scandinavian players, John Jensen and Pal Lydersen.

Scandal and sleaze became the winter's buzz words. Amid the disquiet, came renewed outbreaks of football hooliganism, firstly just a few flames at Millwall and Chelsea, and a referee being chased by a fan at Blackburn, then a forest fire when rioting England fans halted an international in Dublin. Cantona's action at Selhurst Park seemed to light the fire, though clearly he could not be held responsible for all the ills of the game. It did, however, add to the atmosphere of a game in crisis. Later in the season a Crystal Palace supporter, running from a fight with United fans, would die under the wheels of a coach in a pub car park. The rival sets of supporters had been taunting each other with Cantona chants. Someone cleverly and accurately described it as Four Wednesdays and a Funeral.

This was a game with an identity crisis. It had more money than it had ever known, thanks to £304 million from Sky Television, and more attention than ever, thanks to a press becoming more intrusive due to a burgeoning public demand. You sensed, too, that Eric Cantona was enduring an identity crisis. 'He has lost any capacity of judgement on himself,' Erik Bielderman told me. 'When I saw him after Crystal Palace, I thought he was closing to himself, just acting when he was talking. Not any more a person.'

It was one of many views I gathered for *The Red and the Black*. Gérard Houllier, technical director of French football and former national team manager, described Cantona to me as: 'An island of pride and generosity. Somebody who inspires respect, who doesn't talk much but is very friendly.' Somebody else, unwilling to be identified with the remark, but closely associated with him, saw him as: 'A champagne socialist, the antithesis of a sportsman, into all this Jean-Jacques Rousseau "Noble Savage" crap.'

There were as many views as there were, it seemed, Eric Cantonas. But, really, there was only one starting point. 'I am proud that they talk about me,' Eric Cantona once said, 'whether it's good or bad.' So here goes.

2 Night of the Chameleon

They've caught him. Now what name trembles
On his silent lips? What quick regret?
No one will know: the Emperor's eye is dead.
Arthur Rimbaud, 'Angry Caesar'

Manchester United do not play ordinary football matches. For England's biggest club every game is a big game. They have the largest support in the country, drawn from every nook and cranny of the British Isles and beyond: supporters' clubs are registered in 119 countries. It has to do with a culture, a commitment to a playing style that demands success with style. It has, also, to do with a heritage, a mythology, one that rose from the ashes of the Munich air tragedy in 1958, when eight of the Busby Babes, Sir Matt Busby's exciting young team, were cut down on the threshold of greatness.

Wednesday 25 January, 1995, however, was about as ordinary as they come for United – Crystal Palace away – even though the south London club's largest home gate of the season, 18,224, was in position. That was pretty standard; most clubs enjoy a windfall when United are the visitors, not only due to the increased number of local fans but also because many of United's admirers from afar can actually get in – Old Trafford being permanently sold out. On this damp winter's night at Selhurst Park, United were seeking to advance their case for a third consecutive Championship. Palace knew they would be involved in another relegation struggle, but it was not yet desperation time.

What followed, though, was anything but ordinary. For sheer sadness the date will never rank with 6 February, 1958, but for sheer madness it'll be recalled as one of the most notorious incidents in United's history, in English football, in world sport.

Despite the impenetrability of south London, many people braved the journey to the hinterland of the Premiership for the first chance to see Andy Cole, the striker who had joined nine days earlier from Newcastle United in a British transfer record deal worth £7 million. Would Cole score his first goal for his new club? The chief football writers of the national newspapers had turned up hoping to report just such a thing in a match they might otherwise have left to their No. 2s. They were to be glad they had not.

Cole showed few signs in a scrappy and uneventful first half, struggling to integrate with colleagues more used to playing one-two passes with the omitted Mark Hughes than playing the ball over a defence for a striker to run on to. The combative United midfielder Paul Ince was involved in a committed duel with Palace's Darren Pitcher. Eric Cantona was a subdued figure, largely failing, in the face of some tight marking by Richard Shaw, to impose his touch and personality on the game.

'I remember thinking during the first half that Cantona was looking distinctly unhappy,' says Paul Newman, sports editor of the *Independent*, who was watching the match from the stand with his nine-year-old daughter Katy. 'Palace were not violent or dirty but kept a tight rein on him, and Shaw is a good marker. Cantona was getting fed up but I don't remember a single bad tackle. He was not getting a torrid time by my reckoning.'

Twelve minutes into the second half Cantona's frustration surfaced. After a tangle with Shaw he struck out but missed, and the incident went unseen by the referee Alan Wilkie, the ball finding its way to the United goalkeeper Peter Schmeichel. The giant Dane's clearance was dropping near Cantona and Shaw, their arms entangled in a challenge for the ball. Cantona now kicked at

Shaw's legs. Wilkie had seen this one. Cantona was shown the red card. The ritual gathering of players around the incident to swap opinions ensued.

'There was no doubt in my mind that violent contact had been made and no doubt that Cantona had kicked or attempted to kick an opponent,' Alan Wilkie later told *Four Four Two* magazine. 'To his credit, Cantona showed no protest. The look on his face told me he knew exactly what he'd done.' After Cantona had been shown the card, it was a mere 51 seconds before play restarted. There have been so many slow motion replays since, it seems that what followed occupied an age. Wilkie himself saw little, he said, but sat open-mouthed in the dressing room when told afterwards. That night he would not leave the ground until 11.45 p.m., the latest he had ever departed a stadium.

The sending off was nothing new: Cantona's fifth dismissal since his transfer from Leeds United for a knock-down £1 million, which reflected the gamble the club was taking, given his history. After a moment of bemusement, injustice written on his face, Cantona plodded towards the sideline with the weariness that overcomes players in high dudgeon. Only in hindsight is there any amusement, and the Kenneth Williams line from an old *Carry On* film recalled: 'Infamy! Infamy! They've all got it in for me.' Right then, it was sombre stuff. Cantona looked towards the United dug-out for some sympathy, some reassurance from Alex Ferguson, his manager–mentor. There came none. In return, Cantona was his tormentor. Ferguson, his hands in his coat pockets, avoided all eye contact. Perhaps he was just looking elsewhere to reorganize the team. Perhaps not. 'I think Alex was trying to stare the referee out,' the then Crystal Palace manager Alan Smith later told me.

'It looked like Cantona was going to walk to the bench, but I think he saw that Fergie was livid,' said Henry Winter, football correspondent of the *Daily Telegraph*, watching from the press box. Instead, Cantona began to make his way to the dressing rooms via the players' tunnel, set in a corner of the ground. It necessitated a walk of some 50 yards along the touchline. Within touching distance of the crowd.

'The atmosphere got hotter and hotter,' says Paul Newman. 'I remember thinking at the time he started going that someone should go with him. It's a long walk and there was a lot of noise. I heard people shouting things you hear at any ground when the opposition's star player is sent off – "Off, off, off" – that sort of thing. Most people were waving and singing goodbye, some had sarcastic smiles on their faces. It was not pleasant, but it was not unusual.' In fact, Norman Davies, the Manchester United kit man, did go with Cantona, probably because he had the keys to the dressing room.

Then it happened.

Rather than trudging, head bowed, as ordinary players do in such circumstances, Cantona now strode, erect, seemingly resolved to face it with defiant dignity. He had gone some 20 yards when something in the front row of the crowd attracted his attention. He turned and paused, then moved on a few yards. Someone else now disturbed him. There was what seemed to be a spasm of anger, and suddenly he launched himself, right foot first, into a kung-fu kick that has been replayed on television more times than the David Carradine drama series of that name. 'In every picture I have seen since,' says Henry Winter, 'Cantona's eyes are closed. Sharks do that when they go in for the kill.'

Cantona's studded sole landed in the chest of a spectator wearing light trousers, a leather jacket, white shirt and Crystal Palace club tie. Then Cantona fell on to the barrier and on to the ground, before he picked himself up to land a right-handed haymaker, which the spectator returned. The flurry was brief, as are punched exchanges when the adrenalin suddenly rushes through the body to a brain beginning to think better of it. Norman Davies rushed to grab Cantona with the help of a steward who had moments earlier been urging the fan involved to back off.

'And as Cantona walks from the field,' bellowed Capital Radio's stentorian voice of football, Jonathan Pearce, over the airwaves of London, his tones probably even carrying to Manchester on the wind, 'he's . . . Oh my goodness . . . Cantona has . . . This is quite unbelievable . . . He's . . . And now the crowd are . . .

In all my years of commentating I have never seen anything quite like this.'

No one had. Of course one read about incidents in far-away countries of players assaulting, even shooting, referees; of confrontations between players and supporters. There had been the case of Brian Clough cuffing a pitch invader at Nottingham Forest in what was described as a case of the shit hitting the fan. 'Amongst your friends down the pub you never even talked among yourselves about such a thing happening,' says Paul Newman.

'It was so un-English that I wonder whether this was what got everybody so indignant and outraged about it,' says David Meek, the recently retired United reporter for the *Manchester Evening News*. 'I was left wondering if had he come over to the crowd and punched him on the nose, fought with him in a more particularly British way, whether quite such a fuss would have been made of it and any punishment been less expensive.'

Now all hell broke loose and players rushed to intervene. Paul Ince, his fiery nature displayed even when there was no ball to be contested, became involved in the scene. Eventually Cantona was bundled away in the albatross arms of the United goalkeeper Peter Schmeichel, Davies in attendance.

'There was just the sickening sight of a man losing complete control of himself,' says Alan Smith. 'It lasted about twenty seconds, not enough time for me to get there. I didn't want to anyway, though my players said they rushed there because they were worried about friends in the crowd nearby. After that, the whole place was just stunned. We didn't play after that. If anything, United played better than they had been doing.'

The Crystal Palace press box is among the coldest in the league (a joke was that it should have been transported to the white-hot World Cup in the United States), and journalists now had a chance to get the circulation going as they scrambled desperately to share accounts of what had happened, running from there to the police control centre where Chief Inspector Terry Collins of the South Norwood force gave his immediate, stunned, reaction. 'There was potential for a riot. I've never seen anything like it in football.' The game was all but forgotten, David May's goal for United, equalized for Palace by Gareth Southgate, almost irrelevances. Andy Cole missed a good chance.

The Football Association's director of public affairs, David Davies, was at the match and reacted instantly to the media. 'Such an incident brings shame on those involved as well as, more importantly, the game itself,' he intoned carefully. 'The FA is aware that the police are urgently considering what action they should take. We will as always [a statement which reflected football's growing entanglement with the law] co-operate in every way with them.'

The United dressing room was in shock, the players sombre and bemused. Cantona sat in silence, though this was nothing unusual. He often preferred his own company, his own thoughts. What was unusual, though, was that he was still sitting in his kit when the players returned after the final whistle. Ferguson, his face flushed with anger, could barely bring himself to speak. Certainly not to the press. He went for a brief drink to a small private bar in the ground with Alan Smith. 'He was just incredibly shocked,' says Smith. 'He never once commented on the Cantona thing. We talked about the game, he said he thought we would avoid relegation. There was me feeling sick and him thinking "What am I going to do about all this?"'

'I only saw the aftermath, a punch being thrown,' Ferguson was later to say. He thought there might have been fighting in the crowd. 'Then I saw Eric lying over a hoarding and I thought maybe he'd been dragged into the crowd or something. I didn't fully understand how serious it was that night, even having spoken to the police.' He would do just before dawn, which is always the darkest time.

The United party headed swiftly to the airport for a flight to Manchester, arriving back at Ringway just after midnight. Little conversation interrupted the flight. Ferguson is not the most approachable of people after bad nights for United, nor does he like to approach others. Cantona made his way back to his typically ordinary rented home at Worsley, Greater Manchester, some distance from his colleagues' places in Cheshire. His pregnant wife Isabelle, if not exactly waiting with a rolling pin as if for some drunk late home from the pub, read him the Gallic equivalent of the riot act, it would later emerge. He probably spent an uncomfortable night, though probably not one as uncomfortable as Ferguson's.

'It was only when I got home and my son Jason asked if I wanted to watch the video of it,' he later told Jean-Philippe Leclaire of *L'Équipe* magazine. 'I said, "I'll watch it tomorrow," but when I went to bed I couldn't sleep. At five a.m. I got up and watched it. Jesus Christ. It was terrible. I couldn't believe it. How could Eric have done it? At the club he is usually so calm. He often arrives for training half an hour before the others, leaves half an hour after and signs all the autographs the fans want.'

At 8.30 a.m. Ferguson took a call from David Meek. He did not wish yet to be quoted, but voiced fears, for Meek's background to the story, that this was the end for Cantona. Rather it was just the beginning.

As soon as offices opened, the phone lines were humming. David Davies and Graham Kelly, the FA's chief executive, were on the phone to the United chairman and chief executive Martin Edwards. He gave them assurances that Cantona would be dealt with harshly. The FA, according to their own rules, were powerless to act in advance of a disciplinary inquiry, but left Edwards in no doubt that a ban should immediately be imposed. There would be a statutory fourteen days for Cantona to respond to the charge of misconduct and bringing the game into disrepute.

Cantona, meanwhile, was saying nothing. He emerged from his home unshaven, with hair standing up, eyes bleary, wearing jeans and a garish blue, red, yellow and black woolly jacket. He had nothing to offer a phalanx of reporters and photographers save a look of haughty disdain and a smile playing on his lips. He climbed into his M-registered Honda to go to the United training ground, whither, along with Paul Ince, he had been summoned by Ferguson. When he returned a few hours later, all he would say was: 'Be careful what you write.' The silence contrasted with the clamour that was being played out in the tabloids.

On the Friday the *Sun*, barometer of the British bloke, devoted twelve pages to the episode and its repercussions, with more and more details of the real story emerging. They had even signed up the spectator involved, a 20-year-old window fitter from Thornton Heath, Surrey, by the name of Matthew Simmons, for a sum variously reported between £20,000 and £80,000. That added another dimension to the whole sordid story and twisted morality: insult a player, spark a disturbance and get paid a fortune for the whole thing. A nonentity could become notorious in these days of the public wising up to the ways of the media. We had moved from kiss and tell to kick and sell.

The previous day rumours had spread through Wapping and Canary Wharf that Simmons had a six-inch gash to his chest and severe bruising to his face. A police statement containing the fact that there were no serious injuries, only minor bruising, was all but overlooked. 'Cantona's boot studs slammed into my heart' read the *Sun*'s front-page headline. An alternative bare breast on page three duly revealed little in the way of marks or wounds.

'I could see the whites of his eyes – there was total rage in them,' the paper quoted Simmons as saying. 'I reeled back unable to believe what was happening. I was being attacked by one of the biggest soccer stars in the world.' Ooh, the thrill of it. Cantona had come at him like 'an Exocet missile' which is, of course, of French design. 'There were nearly 20,000 people at Selhurst Park, but for those few seconds there might only have been two.' It almost sounded romantic. 'Then,' Simmons continued, 'the crowd came surging forward. I stepped back and held out my hands to protest my innocence.'

Simmons said that he had made the walk eleven rows down to the front of the stand because he wanted to go to the toilet. 'I yelled, "Off you go, Cantona. It's an early shower for you."' Really? Other witnesses recalled something more along the lines of: 'You French bastard. Fuck off back to France, you motherfucker.'

It emerged in newspapers that Simmons had once had connections with extreme right-wing politics, and the previous season at Selhurst Park had been ejected from the ground after his part in a pitch invasion at the end of a match against Watford. And these were among the more savoury aspects of Simmons' past that came out in the papers. The gut feeling that Cantona's action was indefensible was being modified a little, with the question of who was the real victim becoming cloudier. It was clear, however, that no one was entirely innocent. One felt some sympathy for a Mrs Kathy Churchman who was next to the incident with her twelve-year-old daughter Laura. Cantona's lunge had missed Mrs Churchman's face by inches and she was left with stud marks on her coat and leg. Pictures showed her laughing, though, as Simmons was delivering his bile.

On the Thursday night, Ferguson, Martin Edwards, Maurice Watkins (United director and a solicitor) and Sir Roland Smith, chairman of Manchester United plc, met for three hours at Edge Hill Hotel in Alderley Edge, Cheshire, to discuss the situation. The United share price was in the process of falling, the company's valuation having dropped £2.4 million to £77.2 million. Ferguson felt Cantona might have to go. This had to be balanced against the player's contribution to the club – physically and financially in the amount of business his name brought in. Watkins pointed out the legal pitfalls in sacking him. Finally it was decided, in keeping with the impression Edwards had gleaned from his talks with the FA, to ban Cantona until the end of the season and fine him two weeks' wages: £10,800 basically, but probably worth more like £20,000 with bonuses. The verdict was communicated to Cantona and to Gordon Taylor, chief executive of the Professional Footballers' Association. Cantona agreed to it; his consent had to be sought because to deny anyone the right to work for what might be seen as an unfair length of time could be challenged in a court.

The decision was announced at Old Trafford at midday the following day by Watkins. 'In reaching this decision, which the player fully accepts,' he said, before a copious audience that included live Sky Television, 'Manchester United has had regard to its responsibilities both to the club itself and the game as a whole.' He appeared to be using Manchester United as the parent company, rather than just the football club. There were expressions of regret, but an apology from either the club or Cantona was missing. Then again, normally vociferous supporters' organizations such as the Football Supporters' Association were not claiming air time to denounce the behaviour of Matthew Simmons.

The formality over, Edwards expressed the hope that Cantona would be able to play reserve games, but the FA swiftly disabused him of any such idea: they would be seeking a world-wide ban from the game's governing body, FIFA, which was, in due course, granted. The French Football Federation responded by stripping Cantona of the captaincy of the national team and dropping him from international matches for the rest of the season. It was to be expected: the FFF president Claude Simonet was not an ally and had been wondering aloud why Cantona was not the same player for his country that he was for United, though an excellent record of 20 goals in 45 internationals suggested quite a contribution.

Reaction to the punishments was mixed; the issue had split the nation and had become more than any mere football story. Many applauded United's swift action; others felt that Cantona should have been invited to be among the first users of the Channel tunnel. At Old Trafford, former players now turned apologists and pundits, such as Paddy Crerand, trotted out lines about how Manchester United were now being persecuted. The former goal-keeper Alex Stepney was a rare voice of dissent: 'George Best was provoked all the time, but over the years he handled it well,' he said. 'We were brought up to believe that when playing for Manchester United you don't worry about the crowd. There's no escape for Eric Cantona and I don't think he deserves any. He would have been out in Sir Matt Busby's day, to disgrace the club in such a way.' They were simpler, less commercial days, however. Times change and so do standards.

The mood remained fevered, though the Sunday newspapers sought to get behind the story and explain why it might have happened. Cantona, said the *News of the World*, had been 'secretly treated for a speech defect which doctors believe triggers his violent outbursts'. He had once, it added, attended a special school for children where he had to listen to his mother's voice to help overcome his disability. In an interview in the same paper, Alex Ferguson was quoted as saying: 'I sometimes think he is too quiet, shy and unemotional. Maybe he bottles things up to the point where they are liable to burst out disastrously in matches.'

At the front end of the paper, Cantona's mother Eléonore – who had been known to phone up *L'Équipe* in Paris in tears when they had written something about her son with which she disagreed – revealed from the family home in Marseille that her son had telephoned her the morning after the night before, trying not to upset her and her husband Albert, who had been ill with a virus. 'What Eric did was wrong, and of course he knows it,' she said. 'But he was under enormous pressure and after a series of events he just saw red. He said one of the Crystal Palace defenders threw himself at Andy Cole. Eric had tears in his eyes because he was behind Cole and saw it happen. Cole managed to jump out of the way but when you see your partner attacked you're afraid for yourself as well. Then Eric thought when he was given the red card it was perhaps unjustified. Then finally this man in the crowd spat on Eric, made a racist remark and insulted his mother. To insult someone's mother is a very bad thing in France. That does not make what Eric did right, but there is no question of him bringing shame on the family.

'He takes football to heart too much. He always wants to win and if he loses he's very unhappy. Other players in France, not England, don't care if they win or lose, as long as they get paid. But Eric sets goals for himself every year and what happened this week will make him very sad. He recognizes what he did was wrong and it will handicap Manchester United this season. But the club will close around him to support him and I believe they will forgive him because he has so much to give . . . He should not be punished for life for something anyone could have done.'

Not anyone had, though.

Once the hysteria began to die down there was a mellowing of mood, from the outright condemnation to the sympathetic. There was also one thing that had not previously been considered. On his Radio One show, Danny Baker, formerly the splendidly combative host of the Radio 5 football phone-in *Six-o-Six*, asked his sidekick Danny Kelly what should happen to Cantona. 'Immediate pay rise, back on the park,' said Kelly. 'Precisely,' replied Baker. 'I really think the authorities and the media have been out of touch on this one. Most football fans just thought the whole thing was incredibly funny.'

In the *Independent on Sunday*, Richard Williams wrote of the last temptation of Cantona. 'You didn't have to look very long and hard at Mr Matthew Simmons of Thornton Heath to conclude that Eric Cantona's only mistake was to stop hitting him,' went his intro. 'The more we discovered about Mr Simmons, the more Cantona's assault looked like the instinctive expression of a flaw-less moral judgement.'

Cantona had caved in to abuse clearly less vicious than things black players had had to put up with down the years, but Williams made a valid point. 'Acquiring the ability to ignore such systematic abuse is one of the tests of character faced by those who wish to play professional football in England. It is a test that Eric Cantona has clearly failed.' But, he concluded, 'Whatever he did on Wednesday, I don't believe that Eric Cantona is one of the bad guys.'

Old Trafford naturally agreed. On the Saturday, while Cantona took in an art-house movie (*Killing Zoe*) at the Cornerhouse cinema in the centre of the city, United beat Wrexham in the third round of the FA Cup they were defending. The 5–2 victory was played out against a background of 'Ooh-aah, Cantona' chanting. The talk was of getting even with Simmons, and his home address was being circulated. T-shirts bearing the sole of a boot and the message 'I've met Eric Cantona' were on sale. Leaflets were distributed by an opportunistic fringe group, Youth Against Racism in Europe, urging United fans to attend a public meeting concerned with kicking racism out of football. Small boys had their faces painted in United colours, with '*J'aime Cantona*' etched on them.

The following week, at a home Premiership match against Aston Villa, there was even more vibrant support for Cantona, the shock having turned to defiance. The pirate merchandising industry got into full swing – the official one didn't seem to be doing too badly either.

'I do feel that the issues are not quite as simple as some would

have us believe,' wrote Alex Ferguson in the match programme
in his first detailed comment on the Cantona affair, having been
criticized for his restrained reaction to it. 'Football by its very
nature is a very competitive sport and all great teams had players
of aggression and edge. Manchester United in the sixties and
Liverpool of the seventies had volatile men and our present team
is no different. But having said that, I want to make it quite clear
that we can't and won't condone the kind of excess emotion we
witnessed at Selhurst Park. The competition we bring to the game
must be healthy, which is why we had to deal severely with Eric.
It's a punishment he accepts and so we begin life until next season
without the services of our leading scorer and inspirational figure.
I only mention the subject because I wouldn't want anyone to
think we were trying to sweep the situation under the carpet.
There would be little chance of that anyway with the media
enjoying a field day and so many people telling us what we should
and shouldn't do. I believe we have dealt with the case responsibly
and firmly and now we must show that there is life after Eric.'
The Sunday papers would carry the hint of an apology, but contrition still seemed in short supply.

Cantona, meanwhile, was escaping, and escaping criticism. He
should not have been allowed to go home that night, many said:
he should have been detained by South Norwood police. Having
come close to cutting his own throat, he went to Paris to film an
advertisement for the shaving equipment makers BiC. Then he
took off with Isabelle and their son Raphaël for a holiday on the
French West Indian island of Guadeloupe, paid for by United;
another source of criticism.

During his stay he became embroiled in a further remarkable
incident that carried echoes of Selhurst Park. Terry Lloyd, a
reporter with Independent Television News, had been sent to
Guadeloupe to try and secure an interview with Cantona.
Accounts of what occurred were sketchy at the time, and on his
return Lloyd was asked by his employers to pen a memo giving
chapter and verse of his version.

At 9 a.m. on Friday 10 February, Lloyd wrote, he paid to enter
the Club Med complex and saw Cantona enjoying some archery

with Isabelle and Raphaël. When Cantona was finished, Lloyd approached him, shook hands and requested the interview. 'No, I'm on holiday. Do you live here?' Cantona replied and, according to Lloyd, summoned the complex's security men to request Lloyd's removal. Lloyd was allowed to stay within the club for lunch but not allowed to speak to Cantona, who walked by him several times. Lloyd went to the manager to tell him that several newspapers were also about and might remain so. They would all leave if Cantona gave a brief interview. The manager checked with Cantona, who again declined.

The following morning at 10 a.m., Lloyd and his camera crew returned to a public beach next to the Club Med complex and an hour later spotted Cantona and Isabelle sitting at the far end of a jetty. The crew walked to within 40 feet of him and prepared to film. When the camera began rolling, Isabelle, wearing a dark coloured sun dress, was standing up preparing to leave. Her husband glared at the crew, then walked towards them. 'Mr Cantona, when do you intend returning to London?' Lloyd asked. As he repeated the question, not having received an answer, Cantona, his memo said, grabbed him in a head lock. He added that Cantona tried to pull him off the beach towards the complex, saying: 'Come with me. I want to talk to you.' Lloyd replied: 'Come on, Eric, there's no need for violence.'

In Lloyd's account, Cantona then turned his attention to the cameraman, put an arm around his shoulder and attempted to steer him off the beach. Watching security men summoned the manager of the complex and his assistant via walkie-talkies. Soon they appeared, shouting that the film would be confiscated. Lloyd remonstrated, saying that this was a public beach and they had done nothing wrong, then turned to his left to see Cantona. 'He turned, glared at me, ran and launched himself in the air. I saw his feet come up and felt a tremendous blow to my left side. I was flung across the sand, and, as I turned to look back, Eric Cantona was pointing at me, saying: "I'm going to kill you".' As attention turned to the camera crew, Lloyd ran to the hotel reception to phone for the police.

Soon after, Lloyd found his camera crew sitting in a police van.

They had been ordered to hand over the tape under threat of being arrested, and their camera had also been seized. Later, several gendarmes apparently confirmed that the film had been given to Cantona. The police, said Lloyd, who refused to give him their names, were not interested in hearing of Cantona's assault on him. There was one last confrontation for Lloyd. The hotel assistant manager claimed that the crew had not handed over the real tape. Lloyd replied to him that he was in trouble and that, having helped Cantona after he had assaulted him, ITN would be contacting the British and French Embassies and the head office of Club Med. 'What about the Queen, too? No one can save you now,' is Lloyd's recollection of the reply.

Lloyd later endured two sleepless nights and was prescribed pain-killers and ointment for his injured side. An X-ray appeared to show no broken ribs but revealed cartilage damage, and he was prescribed stronger pain-killers. He and his crew were forced to retreat from Guadeloupe, Cantona having benefited from French privacy laws to limit the damage. When Lloyd got back to England, he had another X-ray and this time fractured ribs were confirmed. He also had a neck injury.

'I have heard Manchester United's allegations that we were filming a pregnant woman in a swimsuit on the beach,' said Lloyd. 'Until then, I had not realized that Mrs Cantona was pregnant, and on the three or four occasions I saw her she was always wearing a dress. I would think she hardly featured – if at all – on the tape handed over by the police to Eric Cantona.'

Lloyd, a well-respected and reputable journalist who has covered many major stories, the Oklahoma City bombing among them, is not given to flights of fancy nor falsehoods. The incident clearly happened. Cantona had been fortunate that he had managed to obtain the tape and no film had got out to be shown on the world's screens. He was lucky, too, that the episode had not taken place under British jurisdiction where there is greater freedom of access. There was undoubtedly considerable sympathy for him in being pursued while on holiday – and a statement from Old Trafford pointed out just that while glossing over the incident – but his actions had again been reckless, violent and unnecessary.

Had it been closer to home, it might well have been the final straw.

Cantona returned to England to be interviewed by South Norwood police, who charged him with common assault – in connection with the Selhurst Park incident, that is. There was also the matter of the FA's disciplinary hearing, which was set for Friday 24 February at the Sopwell House Hotel, in a leafy nook on the edge of the small Hertfordshire cathedral city of St Albans. The place, fittingly, was named after a martyr. With its health club, the hotel was used to playing host to football personnel: it frequently billeted teams from the North on the eve of matches in London, Cup Finalists, and international teams taking on England at Wembley. It had seen nothing quite like the mêlée of that day, however.

Cantona, in sombre black suit, grey tie and white shirt, and Ferguson arrived at about 10.30 a.m. to the usual massed clique of photographers, having to push their way through to the hotel entrance. For the next five hours, interrupted by lunch, they and the United solicitor Maurice Watkins sat closeted in a conference room with the three-man committee that comprised Geoff Thompson, chairman of the FA's disciplinary committee, the Oldham Athletic chairman Ian Stott and the Football League president Gordon McKeag.

Journalists milled in the grounds and lounges, kicking heels and drinking coffee, discussing the bribery allegations against Bruce Grobbelaar and George Graham's unsolicited gift. Sky TV broadcast live, every hour, that there was no news yet, just speculation as to what the punishment might be. Bored reporters began to swap anecdotes; one recalled the days of travelling in Europe with a famous English club and receiving a brown envelope from them on check-in as 'spending money'. 'I don't know what I am doing here,' said David Barnes, chief sports writer of the *News of the World*. 'It's probably because I'm the only one in the office who can say in French, "There's two hundred grand for your exclusive story in it for you, Eric."'

Eventually a puff of white smoke went up and all of a sudden Cantona was marching into a room set aside for a press conference. Now he was accompanied by a 'minder', Ned Kelly, a former

SAS man and United's chief security officer. His moustached face and craggy features, which recalled a South African rugby union forward, were to become a familiar sight around Cantona.

Cantona's club ban was to be extended until 30 September and he would be fined a further £10,000, having been found guilty of misconduct and bringing the game into disrepute, Graham Kelly announced. Technically, Cantona was in breach of FA rules. The commission, Kelly added, had taken into account Cantona's previous conduct (or should that have been misconduct), the provocation he had suffered, the prompt action taken by United, Cantona's expression of regret to the commission, the apologies he tendered to those involved and assurances as to his future conduct.

The punishment – which would lead the magazine *When Saturday Comes* to run a front cover of Cantona with a bubble saying: 'I am Eric, my own true self, I am totally free . . . on Saturday afternoons' – seemed a reasonable compromise between the hawks and doves, now that some dust had settled. Kelly was asked, though, if it were not a little light. 'Everyone understands that Eric Cantona faces a court case, has been dealt with by Manchester United, has lost a lot of money, lost the captaincy of the French national team and suffered double the fine he could have suffered in court,' Kelly replied. 'I don't think you could say he has not suffered for his actions. He has come along and said there will be no repetition of this incident. He recognizes the gravity of the situation.'

Kelly went on to touch upon a wider implication for the game, one that would take up much attention in the next few months. 'We're concerned with the increasing level of abuse that footballers have to suffer,' he said. 'We don't think it's acceptable and we do not think it's part of the game. We've already had talks with the Commission for Racial Equality and we hope to speak to leading politicians about a further initiative in this respect.'

Ferguson, sitting on the panel confronted by the arc lights, was asked if he had any comment, but was uncomfortable in the presence of live TV cameras and news reporters rather than the sporting press. He brushed off the thorny question of whether Cantona had received different, better or worse, treatment –

either by Manchester United or the FA – than other, lesser players might have expected. Inside, he was seething that Cantona had been further punished when he thought that the club's own action, taken after negotiations with the FA the morning after it had all happened, would suffice. Maurice Watkins stepped in. 'Naturally disappointed,' was United's reaction, he said. 'A little harsh.'

After a statement read out for the French media by Cantona's lawyer Jean-Jacques Bertrand, the conference was concluded. It had lasted ten minutes, during which time Cantona remained silent, because of the pending court case, it was said. His arms were folded as he looked with amused disdain on the whole gathering. Not one public word of apology did he utter, though to do so might have improved his chances in court. We were assured by Maurice Watkins he had done so in private. How had he apologized? 'Deeply and sincerely,' said Watkins. There were smiles of doubt from journalists, but it probably depended on the intangible definitions of deep and sincere.

'It's a disgrace the way he behaves,' said Erik Bielderman, also in the audience that day. 'Eric always said in interviews that he never regrets what he did, or that he is sorry and wants to excuse himself. I was expecting pressure from the FA or the club for him to make a statement saying, "I am sorry." It is only in a closed room. There he says, "Yes, I am sorry." But he has Manchester United behind him, he has Alex Ferguson, he has his contract, he has his career. I am sure he refused to say sorry in front of the press. He says he doesn't want to talk because of the court case, but this is bullshit. If he had made a statement saying sorry it might help with the case.'

So much was left unsaid; so much about Cantona left to be said. Outside Sopwell House, Gordon Taylor of the PFA wondered aloud to reporters about the state of the game and, with so many bodies administering, who was running it. The Cantona case had climaxed an astonishing month in English football, during which the riot in Dublin had also happened. Cantona still had much to face: a court case with its possibility of imprisonment.

He had also to decide on a move to Internazionale, whose interest, along with the pressure they were putting on Manchester

United, was growing. This was typical of Eric Cantona, who had had preliminary talks about a new contract with Manchester United the day before the Palace match, and knew that representatives of the Italian club were in the crowd at Selhurst Park that Wednesday night. He cared little about the future, even with so much personally at stake, cared so little about impressing people. What was it, though, in his past that made him so, that made the present an echo chamber of all his combined experiences?

3 Enter the Dragon

Into this house we're born,
Into this world we're thrown,
Like a dog without a bone,
An actor out on loan.
The Doors, 'Riders on the Storm'

'1966 was a good year for English football,' read the opening line
on the huge Nike poster. 'Eric was born.' It advertised not only
the sports equipment manufacturer's own products but also one
of their most celebrated clients, who along with John McEnroe,
was similarly filled with a rage for perfection. Out of the billboard,
which was given huge prominence outside Old Trafford, stared
an unshaven face caught in a characteristically lofty expression.

Eric Daniel Pierre Cantona was born on 24 May of that year,
just two months before English football's greatest – indeed, only
– international triumph. He grew up in the cultural melting pot
of Marseille; the environment and sociology of sun and sin was
to shape him. The city's reputation is based on the romance of
the brigand and the reality of the drugs trade. Its people are warm
and have to live with the image of crime and corruption that is
reflected in the eyes of the rest of France.

It also has a grand passion for football and its team, Olympique
de Marseille, which the young Cantona grew up supporting

fervently, has reinforced the stereotype of some style and more corruption. For his part in rigging a match against Valenciennes to enable Marseille to retain the French title in 1993 Bernard Tapie, politician, owner and a man Cantona would later come to despise, was jailed, the club's achievements tarnished. The same season Marseille beat Milan 1–0 in the European Cup. It should have been the finest hour of the nation's club football history.

Like many in Marseille, Cantona was of mixed Mediterranean stock, his paternal ancestors came from the Italian island of Sardinia, his maternal from Spain. The family home – the first example of '*la différence*' in all matters Cantona – was a cave in the hills of the Caillols district, between the 11th and 12th *arrondissements*, overlooking the city, on the edge of Provence. It had been discovered by Cantona's grandmother Lucienne as suitable shelter for her, her husband Joseph, who was a struggling mason, and young son Albert – Eric's father – in 1955. Using his skills Joseph would develop it, building rooms above and around the cave. By the time Eric was born to Albert and his wife Eléonore, three years after Jean-Marie and seventeen months after Joël, it was serviceable; still not large it formed only one room, but was an object of curiosity to the locals.

'The child is father to the man,' wrote William Wordsworth. Even if not entirely conventional, Cantona's childhood appears to have been almost idyllic, with few signs of the unsocial behaviour that was to surface in his professional footballing career. The man who would come to England billed as '*Le Brat*' was no brat, though by all accounts an emotional child. Then again, which child isn't, particularly a third one struggling for attention. And while the family may have been poor, Cantona himself clearly enjoyed his surroundings and closeness to his relatives. 'I am a son of rich people,' he said in his autobiography.

The influences were those of his father Albert (who worked as a psychiatric nurse), namely painting and hunting; the accent that of the Marseillais, one that would be lampooned later on French television's equivalent of *Spitting Image*, *Les Guignols de L'Info*, in which his character is called Picasso, due to his fondness for art. 'But they make fun of everyone on the show. Actually, the

Provençal accent is one we like. It smells of sun, of good food, of olive oil, of the good life,' says Erik Bielderman. 'We like to hear a little bit of the singing accent. The Marseille person has this image of being a little bit of a liar, an over-reacting person. It is a tough city like Liverpool. Provence is the opposite: holidays, food, warm people, and Cantona is sitting between the two. We say he is between two chairs.'

At the age of eight, Cantona was drawn to the attic where his father liked to paint, unlike Jean-Marie, who now owns a sports shop in Marseille, and Joël, also a professional footballer who had spells in England with Peterborough and Stockport County before returning to play for Marseille. Eric described it as 'the other playroom of my childhood. In the daytime there was school and football. In the evening there was the workshop.' He also said in his autobiography: 'In truth, there is no finer childhood than that which is balanced between sport and the imaginary.' Grand-mère Lucienne, whose pizzas Cantona adored, once recalled Eric copying Van Gogh's self-portrait. 'It was better than the original,' said Lucienne, who had proudly hung his first effort – an interpretation of fruit on a plate – above the family television.

Albert Cantona also loved football and was a goalkeeper. He instructed his young son in that form of art, too. 'You don't have to be mad to be a keeper, but it helps,' goes the adage. Cantona *fils* was not mad enough for long enough, however – so those who suspect otherwise will have to look elsewhere for signs – and soon he became an outfield player. 'You start wanting to play football when you are three, four, five years old,' Cantona was later to say in the Manchester United video, *Eric the King*. 'You know you have a passion when you can't stop playing the game, when you play it in the streets and the playground after school, when you spend your time at school swapping photographs of footballers.' He was also to say: 'It has to be said that playing football in the streets gave us a tremendous need for freedom.' He was never to lose it.

He joined the Caillols junior club, which was already celebrated in southern French circles. It had produced Jean Tigana, who, in Cantona's formative years, was held up as role model and inspiration at the club. Tigana was a beautiful, galloping fallow deer of a midfield player who would play alongside Michel Platini – also to play an important part in Cantona's career – in the marvellous France midfield of the 1980s, which also included Alain Giresse. They reached the World Cup semi-finals in 1982 and thrillingly won the European Championship in their own country in 1984.

Dutch football was also a huge influence on le jeune Cantona playing in the streets and local fields. Johan Cruyff was a particular hero, probably after Albert had taken the six-year-old Eric to the Stade Vélodrome and sat him on his shoulders to watch Marseille play Ajax of Amsterdam in a European Cup tie. Eric was charmed by the Dutch reaching the 1974 and 1978 World Cup finals, distraught at them losing both.

'As little kids we were always competing,' recalled frère Joël. 'We would play football all day around the housing estate, with lunch at half-time. I was always Kevin Keegan while Eric was always Johan Cruyff. They were our idols. Even then Eric was special. At six he was already very skilful, very good at overhead kicks and so on, and always good at passing. Of course he won loads of medals.' Joël was never quite the player that Eric became, though the two have remained close. When Joël was with Stockport and Eric was nearby in his early career with Manchester United, the two would often meet to discuss the game into the early hours, even though they were miles apart in status. Once at Stockport, incidentally, the then manager Danny Bergara, a Uruguayan by birth, was questioned at a press conference about his team's long-ball style. 'We have to play this way,' he replied. 'I don't have a Maradona or a Cantona.' 'Yes you do,' said a reporter. 'Joël.'

History lends a rose-tinted spectacle to Joël's memory: Eric was not always such a great passer. The younger brother himself recalls one night being chided by his father for his exhibitionism and selfishness. 'There is nothing more stupid than a footballer who pretends to be more indispensable to the game than the ball,' said Albert. 'Rather than run with the ball, make the ball do the work, give it and look quickly. Look around quickly and you will be the best. There is nothing more simple than football,' he added. 'Look before you receive the ball and then give it, and always remember that the ball goes quicker than you can carry it.' The boy was hurt and chastened and went to bed with tears in his eyes. The words, though, obviously struck home and could be recalled years later when it came to citing important moments that moulded Eric Cantona.

At the Caillols club, Cantona's first coach Aimé Moléro threw him into the third team to stop being badgered. They easily won the local championship and Moléro built his next side around Eric. In an international junior tournament at the club, grand-père Jo recalled: 'He was so brilliant. He asked the coach where he wanted him to play and Motero just told him, "Wherever you want."' It is reminiscent of the time when the great Scottish manager Jock Stein was asked which was Kenny Dalglish's best position: 'Ach, just let him on the park.' 'Eric had a great intelligence on the field,' said Aimé Moléro. 'He was very fast. I told the others to play long balls towards him. As soon as the ball was played to him, it was a certain goal.'

There were occasional outbursts. 'It was obvious that Eric was something special,' Yves Cicculo, the Caillols club president, told Richard Williams for an *Independent on Sunday* profile of Cantona. 'He had all the qualities of a player. At the age of nine, he was playing like a fifteen-year-old. When he was with us, we won lots of tournaments – and I can honestly say that he alone made the difference.' And temperamentally? 'Exactly as he is today. Hot-headed, but a genius. He's always been his own man. I have to admit that he was a little difficult occasionally. He knew he was better than anyone else. And there were sometimes difficulties with the other lads. It wasn't serious. It was all in the cause of his football. And the Eric Cantona that I see on the television today, *c'est bien lui*, he hasn't changed.'

From the Caillols infants school, Cantona went on to the Grande Bastide secondary school in Mazargue where one of his teachers was Célestin Oliver, a former international who had played in the 1958 World Cup finals when France finished third. Oliver became a footballing mentor, convincing Cantona of his ability as a player. He also, according to his pupil, encouraged him to believe in his own individuality and be true to his own character; to express himself forcibly though remembering his place in the team.

He was not an especially bright pupil, even if he was apparently the only one of the three brothers to do his homework. 'Let's say he was in the middle,' recalled Oliver to *Le Sport* magazine. Outdoor pursuits, particularly football, were more his preference and his school reports bemoaned his failure to achieve his academic potential. 'I think he has regretted not pursuing his studies,' Jean-Marie told *Le Sport*. 'Even if he wasn't very keen on them,' Oliver added,' 'he was very intelligent. On the football field, too. Eric didn't play on instinct. With the ball at his feet, he took his time deciding on the best option. He dared to do things with the ball.'

He was clearly always competitive, too. 'Eric always had to win,' said Jean-Marie. 'At table tennis, tennis or football, he could not bear to lose. We often squabbled over small things. He was fairly quiet, in his secret places. His feelings would take him off to his painting and he would place himself in front of a canvas. If it wasn't always pretty, it was certainly powerful.'

If the influences of his father and Célestin Oliver were important to his physical development, that of his mother was obviously apparent in his moral outlook. 'My son never liked injustice,' she said in *Le Sport*. 'I always taught him what was right.' In terms of experiences, there was one at the age of twelve that he was to include in his autobiography and reflect on in *Eric the King*.

Caillols had just won the Provence Cup by beating Vitrolles 3-0 and could also win their league if they avoided defeat in their final match against Vivaux-Marronniers. In the video, it was to the night before the game that he was referring when he said: 'When you wake up in the middle of the night before playing on a Sunday morning to check that no one has stolen your boots, that's passion.'

His team trailed 1-0 with five minutes to go. Then, according to his own recollection, Cantona seized the ball in his own half and, his memory has it, went past six players. He was apparently in the act of drawing back his foot to score what he thought would be the title-winning goal when the whistle blew. His laces were undone and the referee demanded Cantona tie them there and then. At least that was how it appeared to the angry youth. It clearly made a strong impression. 'I learned about how much stupidity and injustice there was all around,' he was to say in the autobiography. That night, he says, he lay in bed gazing up at the poster of his hero on the wall: Bruce Lee.

Two years later, the gateway to a professional career opened up for Cantona. Henri Émile, a South-East representative of the French Football Federation, had come to watch a team in which Cantona was playing, in particular another player about whom he had heard much. 'I can't even remember who it was now. I don't think anything became of him,' Émile told me. 'My attention was immediately drawn to this boy called Cantona.' He had, says Émile, now assistant to the French national coach Aimé Jacquet, an 'allure'.

'He was different. He had more intelligence than the others, was a level above them. He had good technique, spirit and initiative. He knew when to hold the ball, when to pass it, knew how to use it to do positive things.' Émile selected him for the regional team and recommended him to Guy Roux, legendary patriarch of Auxerre football club on the northern tip of Burgundy, 400 miles from Marseille. They had a reputation, the best in the country, for developing young players to their full potential.

Soon Cantona had received an offer from Roux to visit the club and discuss the possibility of a move. The teenager was torn between his roots, his deep attachment to his family, and his desire for a good start to his career. Nice, only some hundred miles to the east along the Côte d'Azur, had spotted him too and invited him along. Célestin Oliver advised him to go there; it appealed, too, to Cantona as the club of two of his early heroes, the French international Roger Jouve, another product of Caillols, and the Pole Ivan Katalinski.

The basis for his career decision was not one that might seem important to more mature people, but clearly it meant a lot to an impressionable fourteen-year-old. On a visit to Nice, Cantona was disappointed not to be given club pennants or a shirt. By contrast, he came back from Auxerre 'loaded with treasures'. Roux gave him a fortnight to go home and think over the move but Cantona was quickly ready with an answer.

His childhood was over. In later life he would say: 'Children are drawn to sincerity and authenticity. The way I work and pursue my career, I don't betray them and they know it. I don't see any good in teaching them to deny their own emotions for the benefit of the established order.' It was how he had grown up.

It was time, he concluded, to fly the nest. His grandfather's family, after all, had come from Sardinia while his grandmother's father had been a freedom fighter in Franco's Spain before fleeing to France. Cantona suspected, too, that the nomadic spirit he felt inside him came from a father who was unable himself to indulge it, with a family to support, but escaped in painting instead. For the first time, but not the last, Eric Cantona acted on instinct. 'I wish I had never had to leave the world of children,' he would one day say. Given how free a spirit he had developed into, his ensuing career was to show in many ways – and he himself would probably deem it a compliment – that he never did.

4 French With Tears

The boy who picked the bullets up, Destiny's child
In whose blood flows the memory of an exiled
Father, now aspires to new stature of his own.
Arthur Rimbaud, 'The Boy Who Picked the Bullets up'

Auxerre is a small, sleepy town of some 40,000 people about a hundred miles south-east of Paris just off the A6 motorway at the tip of the Burgundy region. Years ago people might have stopped there on their way to somewhere else, possibly for a lunch in one of the several fine gastronomic restaurants, to imbibe some of the white wine from the village of Chablis a few miles away. These days, it is almost as well known for its football.

From the depths of the French game, the club has risen to become one of the most consistent in the First Division, frequently reaching European competition and, from this unlikely back-water, producing a stream of young players. They have also developed facilities that are the envy of big city clubs. It is almost entirely due to one man, Guy Roux, probably the world's longest serving professional club manager.

Roux arrived at Auxerre in 1962 to take on the job with a club then in the Third Division and attracting gates of around 200. He was a novice coach, who claims to have played once upon a time for Crewe Alexandra, and was hired by the club's chairman, then and still, Jean-Claude Hamel, a lorry salesman. 'At first our aim was simply to go up a division,' said Hamel. Roux had an altogether grander vision: 'From the start I saw the club as an empty set for a great film. All I had to do was direct it.'

The main feature emerged. With the support of a proud municipality, the stadium was gradually developed, along with training fields around it. A centre of excellence was established, where apprentices lived in. In 1991 two young England schoolboys, Jamie Forrester and Kevin Sharp, who later went on to Leeds, even decided that, educationally, this was the best place to begin their professional careers. Back in 1979 Roux had led Auxerre to a French Cup Final against Nantes. The following year they reached the First Division for the first time.

It was into this flourishing environment that Cantona came in May 1981, having just celebrated his fifteenth birthday at home in Caillols. He adapted well enough, though was often homesick. He kept a picture of his parents above his bed in his lodgings. Cantona's grandmother Lucienne has told how she would sometimes receive telephone calls from the woman concierge who had found him sobbing alone. On his trips back home, he would indulge his fondness for Lucienne's pizza to the extent that Roux would joke on his return that he was putting on weight and losing speed.

Roux was to describe Cantona as 'the most brilliant of our youth trainees' and would later say: 'I remember we had a meal with his mother and grandmother when he joined us. And I told them, "He will play for France." He was like a matchstick, but he had class and he saw the game very clearly. He was always trying things. When they came off, it was magnificent – but often they didn't and he gave the ball away. That was his principal fault. We had to teach him more discipline. He was mischievous, sometimes difficult, but children at that age are. There was nothing we couldn't deal with.'

The following spring, even though at this stage Cantona was only a fourth-team player, Roux pitched him into a training game against the club's first team, including their star Polish striker Andrej Szarmach. It was one of Roux's little ruses, designed to keep the feet of the first team on the ground. Cantona came on for the second half and proceeded to give the centre-back Lucien Denis an uncomfortable time. 'Off balance, the defender tried to foul me at every opportunity,' Cantona recalled.

The experience may have had something to do with Denis's sour recollections of the precocious youth. Later he would remember a reserve team match against Melun when Cantona was involved in a tough physical contest with an opposing defender. Denis says that as they were leaving the ground, the defender asked Cantona if he had calmed down yet. Cantona was apparently not amused. Denis, now a newsagent, also recalls once ribbing Cantona about wearing sunglasses and being afraid of the sun; again Cantona seems not to have seen the funny side.

By the next season, Cantona had risen to the third team and won selection for the French national youth side, for a match against Switzerland in Lyon. It would be a curtain raiser to the France v Bulgaria qualifier for the World Cup in Spain. Inspired by sharing the same hotel with his heroes, the likes of Platini, Tigana and Giresse, Cantona went on to score the third goal in a 3–2 win.

At seventeen I learned the truth, sang Janice Ian. For Cantona, it was certainly a significant year. Now with the reserves, his playing career was going well, and he would end the season with 20 goals as Auxerre's team in the Third Division – for reserve teams – won the title. He was second top scorer behind Bernard Ferrer, who had arrived at the club from Vichy. It was fortuitous for Cantona, as Ferrer introduced his sister Isabelle to him. He was smitten by the sophisticated student of literature and commerce at the University of Aix-en-Provence, who, at twenty, was three years his senior. A relationship that was to blossom into marriage began with Isabelle often travelling to Auxerre in her vacations, to stay with Bernard but to be with Eric.

There was, too, a less happy moment. The growing legend of Cantona was to be fuelled by a story that, after one ill-tempered reserve match, he had been confronted by seven opponents in the car park outside the Auxerre ground. Four of them, the tale had it, needed hospital treatment. 'Eric was just a guy, like the rest,' said his room-mate on away trips, William Prunier. 'He was very shy. He confided only in those who knew him well. I think he was maturing in his game and in himself. His turbulent side, which I saw in the training camp when he broke table-tennis bats because he didn't like losing, was gradually disappearing.' For a while, anyway.

That autumn, Cantona was given his initial taste of first-team football, in a match against Nancy, and also went on to play against Lens. At the end of the season, however, Cantona having reached his eighteenth birthday, Roux decided that it would be best for him to get his compulsory one-year's national service out of the way. With Ferrer, he joined the Joinville battalion, reserved for sportsmen, at Fontainebleau, near Paris, and even played for the French army team, enjoying a week in Gabon, West Africa. It was, said the completely non-military Cantona 'a formidable school of fun', and he and Ferrer do not appear to have stinted on the night life.

They even, by Cantona's own admission, carried it over for a while when they returned to Auxerre. Cantona had scored his first senior goal for the club against Rouen on 14 May, 1985, then was included in the team that needed a point from a match in Strasbourg to qualify for the UEFA Cup. Ferrer and Cantona, on the eve of the match, took the opportunity for a night out that finished at 4 a.m. Cantona scored the equalizer in a 1-1 draw.

His hope of playing European football the following season was dashed. Auxerre were drawn against AC Milan, and Roger Boli, brother of Basile of Marseille and Glasgow Rangers, retained his place in the side that Cantona had vacated after a bout of flu. Auxerre, remarkably, won the first leg 3-1 but lost 3-0 in the San Siro, Mark Hateley scoring one of the goals and Cantona making only a token appearance as a substitute.

Roux suspected Cantona's mind was elsewhere and even telephoned Isabelle Ferrer in Aix-en-Provence to determine how serious was her relationship with Cantona. It was serious. Roux duly offered Cantona on loan to Martigues, then a small Second Division club near Marseille who have since gone on to become the Wimbledon of France, sustaining a place in the First Division on gates of a few thousand. The French Second Division was of a decent standard, something akin to the lower end of the Football League's First Division, and Cantona's skills would stand out, his physical development be enhanced.

Cantona jumped at the chance, loaded up his Peugeot 104 and took up residence with Isabelle in her tiny one-bedroom flat. Football became almost an afterthought as the two of them enjoyed the life of a couple. 'Incidents' still followed him, though. In a match against Grasse in December, Cantona was sent off for a *coup de grâce* of his own, then a disagreement developed in the stand, where sat his brother Jean-Marie, upset by remarks directed towards Eric. In trying to leap a fence, Jean-Marie bloodily cut his hand. Cantona himself went over to see what was happening, before being led away.

He was also sent off in a match against Cannes, but by and large it seems to have been a happy time for player and club. 'Guy Roux sent him to us as a "joker", for him to rediscover his physical and moral health,' said Jean Patti, then vice-president of the club. 'We were bottom of the table when he played his first match against Montceau. He scored and it lifted the whole club.' He was to score only three more goals in fifteen appearances but the club was more than happy with his other contributions. A team picture of the time shows him wearing white gloves, like some magician. 'He was withdrawn, but I think he was happy here,' said Patti.

At the end of the season, Roux was worried anew that he might be losing his protégé to the South. He travelled to Lyon to watch Cantona play for Martigues and to tell him that he would be offered a full professional's contract. Cantona was ready to return. That summer of '86, he and Isabelle were married – sending out notices of their nuptials after the event – and made a home in Yonne, some 20 kilometres from Auxerre, near the woods of Poilly where he could hunt woodcock and walk his dogs. He was about to impose himself on the French First Division at the age of twenty. Under Roux, Auxerre were developing a reputation for neat, fluent football with the emphasis on passing and movement. They lacked, however – in common with much of French football – a physical aggression. The manager saw in Cantona just such. And should he blend the aggression with the technique, he would have something rare, something he had been missing.

Cantona loved to be noticed and was determined to make an impact. On the eve of a match in Brest he had his head shaved 'to feel the fresh rain and the strength of the wind on my skull'. It was his goalscoring, however – 13 in the season – that got him noticed by the French Under-21 selectors and he became part of an exciting group which was to reach the final of the European Championship.

In a group match against the Soviet Union he headed France into the lead and, after an equalizer, claimed the winner. In the semi-final against England, who had among their number Paul Davis and Chris Fairclough, he led France to an astonishing 4–2 win in the home leg, the highlight being a crossfield backheel that threw the England defence and opened space for Stéphane Paille to drive a beautiful goal. Then in the return at Highbury Cantona scored both goals in a 2–2 draw, drawing the attention of English coaches. It seems to have been among the happiest times of his career. 'There was a great team spirit and I think we realized we were gifted,' he was to say. 'We played football with a total free-dom as if we were children with few cares. And we were great friends. Without friendship in football, you won't go far, even if you are gifted.'

Now Cantona was making waves at the top level in France, but he was not so arrogant that he would not help clear snow one winter's morning from the Auxerre pitch. He resented, however, that the first-team goalkeeper Bruno Martini was not pulling his weight, and remarked just such to him. Martini took exception and felt the force of a Cantona right-hander that blacked his eye. Martini was, thus, both shaken and stirred. Cantona was fined heavily by the club. 'That temperament from the South,' said Guy Roux, 'it makes you have bad moments.'

Soon Cantona was a full international himself, called up by Henri Michel for a friendly against West Germany in Berlin. Michel was not especially impressed even though Cantona scored France's only goal just before half-time – one that resembled Gary

Lineker's for England in the World Cup semi-final against Germany in 1990 – in response to two early ones by Rudi Völler in a 2–1 defeat. He left the field furious at the result. Cantona would win only four more caps in two years under Michel and would later be involved in a public disagreement with the manager that would cost him dearly.

It was at around this period that Cantona also underwent psychoanalysis, though it seems it was a consciousness-raising experiment on his part rather than a response to any suggestion he needed treatment for his volatility. 'I was at liberty to begin a session of psychoanalysis without being called a madman,' said Cantona. 'I had started seeing [a psychoanalyst] because of my interest in the subconscious . . . it wasn't a question of being worried about my state of mind.'

By April 1988 Cantona was getting itchy feet, and matters were not improved when he was sent off against Nantes for a dangerous tackle – his tackling was to be a recurring weakness through his career – on Der Zakarian, for which he was suspended for three matches. His apprenticeship long over, 81 first-team appearances and 23 goals behind him, he felt ready for a change. After Auxerre had lost to Lille in a French Cup quarter-final, he asked for a transfer. Roux put it down to the immediate disappointment of youth, but Cantona was more serious than that.

Matra Racing of Paris and his home-town club of Marseille, now under the control of the tycoon and politician Bernard Tapie, were immediately interested. There was even talk of AC Milan taking an interest, though whether this was genuine or just Cantona's new agent Alain Migliaccio fermenting interest was open to question. Cantona's psychoanalyst advised him to try England. Right advice, perhaps; wrong time.

Cantona was impressed by the Parisian president Jean-Luc Lagardère, notably his interest in painting and possession of a work by Miro, but plumped for Marseille, initially impressed by Tapie and unable to resist the prospect of returning to his home-town club in glory. It would not always be so. 'I wanted to experience what my idols had experienced,' said Cantona. The transfer fee was 22 million Francs, at the time some £2.3 million,

a French record. Cantona would be receiving a salary twenty times
that he was getting at Auxerre.

The popular perception is that the patriarchal Roux handled
Cantona better than any of the other six club managers in France
for whom Cantona subsequently played. But there may have been
some relief for Roux in selling him. 'He had some problems
with Eric, I think,' said Gérard Houllier when we met at the
offices of the French Football Federation in Paris. 'I don't think
he would like to speak to you about Eric. At that time Eric
was not as mature as he is now. Even mature he has his difficult
side.'

Is it fair to say that Roux found him a handful? 'Oh yes. Because
Eric is a character. But he was very young and very strong, and
Guy was a strong character himself. He pumped a lot of time and
energy into Eric, and sometimes you put more time and energy
into one person than you do into the rest of the team.' Erik
Bielderman's perception is: 'Roux was afraid of Eric. Physically
and mentally he couldn't control him. Guy Roux doesn't like
keeping a player he can't control.'

French football had been looking for a star for a long time.
After Just Fontaine, who scored 13 goals at the World Cup finals
of 1958 in Sweden – a record unlikely to be beaten – the game
had endured a long, colourless period. The French had also
developed a huge inferiority complex in international competition.
The European Cup had been their idea – that of a sports writer
on L'Équipe – and Reims had reached the first Final in 1961. But
when Cantona joined Marseille in 1988, no French club had won
a European trophy; English clubs in that time had won 21. French
football was always full of skilful players but was often found
wanting in mental fortitude.

In the mid-seventies Dominique Rocheteau and St Etienne
arrived on the scene. Rocheteau – 'the green angel' – was France's
answer to George Best: all mazy dribbles, flowing long hair, and
guitar waiting to be strummed in the dressing room. Michel
Platini added guile to the grace and in 1976 they reached the
European Cup Final, only to lose 1–0 to Bayern Munich in
Glasgow.

Their domestic domination was followed by that of Bordeaux, resplendent in their purple kit, as their President Claude Bez broke the bank chasing an elusive European Cup. It was a costly failure and Bez was subsequently jailed for fraud. Monaco picked up the baton and attempted to compete with the cream of Europe, signing the Englishmen Glenn Hoddle and Mark Hateley. They, too, ultimately failed at the top level. The problem was money, with the French game veering between boom and bust. It did not have the bedrock of gate money that England and Italy had, with attendances low in many places, watching teams often defensive away from home, and without the culture of come-rain-come-shine support. Funding often came from wealthy benefactors and egomaniacs, sponsorship, television and municipalities. Much of it was transitory, however.

All this was not going to stop Bernard Tapie from trying to capture the European Cup, though. Marseille had always been one of France's bigger clubs, with one of the few sets of loyal supporters. But they were also great under-achievers. Tapie, of course, would succeed, but it would all end in tears, the European Cup being withdrawn. Back in 1988, Cantona was a sign of Tapie's ambition.

Marseille is everything that Auxerre is not: vibrant, hot and passionate. The fever for football from a population some fifteen times the size of Auxerre is intense. Like Liverpool, culturally. Chris Waddle, who joined the club from Tottenham Hotspur in July 1989 for a then enormous £4.25 million, agrees. 'Yes, but in football terms they're more like Newcastle really. Passionate. Liverpool have always been at the top – Newcastle have had three or four years here, three or four there. That's Marseille. I always felt it could go at any moment, that it wasn't based on very much. I remember Franz Beckenbauer trying to make the club more professional, but I had to take my own training kit home and wash it. Marseille is not the best place in the world – it's old, it's dirty in places – but the fans were fantastic. It's an intimidating place to come. Every game in my three years there was a sell-out. You could tell teams coming there were petrified. It was very aggressive. I remember speaking to some Milan players after we played them in the European Cup and they were telling us they were quite scared.

'When I was there, everyone wanted to beat Marseille, like they do with Manchester United in England now. Before them, it was Liverpool. Tapie was a powerful man and people liked to see him beaten. I always got on well with him, but maybe that was because I was naive. If he said something that I didn't agree with, then I said so. He said that Eric would be the new Platini, and there was a lot of pressure on Eric to produce the goods, but maybe he was too young and inexperienced to realize that.' Indeed, the burden of being the great white hope, goalscorer and creator, on the home boy was to come too soon with Marseille's renaissance in its infancy.

Cantona's career at the Stade Vélodrome began inauspiciously. He failed to score in the first five matches of the season and that August was not included in the national squad for a match against Czechoslovakia. The night before the announcement he had scored his season's opener, against Matra Racing, and three days later another two goals against Strasbourg in a 3–2 win. He now felt qualified to voice his opinion of Henri Michel.

'I will never play for France again as long as Henri Michel is manager,' he said in an emotional television interview. 'I would like it to be known that I think he is one of the most incompetent managers in world football. I was reading an article by Mickey Rourke, who's a guy I really like, that the people who award the Oscars are a bunch of shitbags [*sacs à merde*]. I think Henri Michel is not far from being included in that.'

The following day, seeing himself on television, Cantona regretted his words, calling them 'clumsy', but they earned him, after a Federation disciplinary hearing three weeks later, a ban of a year from all international football. The most distressing part of which, to Cantona, was being unable to play in the second leg of the European Under-21 Championship Final against Greece, having helped the team to a 0–0 draw in the away leg. Cantona's opinion of Michel as a good player – indeed an excellent one in midfield for Nantes in the 1970s – but a bad manager seemed soon to be substantiated by the French Federation. Michel was sacked the next month, October, and replaced by Michel Platini, who wanted the wayward sheep back in the fold as soon as possible.

Meanwhile with Marseille Cantona was struggling to find his form, justify his fee, and live up to the great expectations. He had scored only five goals in 22 matches. A feeling was growing that he had made a mistake in returning, one that he voiced in later years: 'I was overawed by the atmosphere,' he confessed. 'It was such a powerful change. I couldn't quite work out what was expected of me. Going back, seeing all my relatives and friends, put me back in the past. I slipped back ten years, went back to my amateur days.'

His frustration boiled over at a charity match in Sedan. Playing against Torpedo Moscow in a game for the Armenian earthquake disaster fund, he responded to whistling and jeering from the crowd by kicking the ball on to the terraces, hurling his shirt at the referee and storming off the pitch after being substituted. Tapie imposed an immediate, indefinite suspension.

While the controversy continued in Marseille, Cantona went to Barcelona to stay with a friend. He returned to find that the coach Michel Hidalgo, who had been manager of that French team at the World Cup of 1982, was ready to loan him to Bordeaux for the rest of the season. Tapie, who said that Cantona might be better going to a clinic, added that Cantona would never play for the club again. 'A player who throws his shirt to the ground must be sanctioned. This does not correspond to my idea of football at Marseille,' he said.

'From what I heard when I joined the club, I think a lot of people were laughing at Tapie,' says Waddle. 'He always wanted to see a happy ship, and be in control and call the shots. But when something like that happens, the publicity goes the other way and people say: "Look, you paid that for him and he's thrown his shirt off," or "Look, he can't play that well, he's not that good on the pitch."'

French television hired a psychiatrist to analyse Cantona for a programme. His conclusion was that in a game that was sick, he was honest, intelligent and an individual. He rather approved of Cantona's statement: 'I am happy to be crazy. The world in which we live is boring. Anyone who is different from the ordinary is considered crazy. I express myself without thinking. I say what I feel.' There was, meanwhile, a hint of contrition from Cantona regarding his shirtiness. 'By throwing away my shirt I was wrong,' he said. 'But only in terms of the image it created of me and in terms of my career.' He did not, he added, regret that he had not fulfilled expectations at the Stade Vélodrome. He would return, he insisted.

Cantona left Marseille airport – so long, Marignane – and was delighted to be met at Bordeaux's Merignac by Jean Tigana, now coach to the Girondins, who were seeking to resurrect themselves from Claude Bez's ashes, having worked their way up again after relegation for financial irregularities. Clive Allen had come from Tottenham and gone again after failing to produce the goods; perhaps Cantona could. The initial signs were good as he scored six goals in 11 games, playing as an out-and-out striker. There followed, though, another incident that soured a club against him. This, in comparison, seemed to be storm-in-a-teacup stuff. One morning Cantona found one of his dogs prostrate, seriously ill, and attended to it rather than report for training. Over-reacting somewhat, Didier Couécou, the assistant to the Bordeaux president, said: 'You must be on your guard against his acts of truancy.'

At the end of his four-month loan spell, Cantona returned to Marseille and was promptly loaned again, surprisingly, for a year to Montpellier, about 80 miles along the coast to the west. It would mean a 50 per cent pay cut but he was grateful to get away from Marseille.

He was also excited by the prospect of linking up with Stéphane Paille, a colleague from the French Under-21 team that had so excited Cantona, and who had recently signed from Sochaux. The partnership and the team did not gel, however, and they made a poor start to the season. By the end of September a relegation struggle looked to be developing, rather than the expected challenge for a UEFA Cup place.

The frustration, again, was to get to Cantona. In the dressing room, after a defeat at Lille, he overheard team-mate Jean-Claude

Lemoult voicing the opinion that the team's problems were down to the strikers. Cantona, incensed, threw his boots in Lemoult's face and a fight ensued. A petition against Cantona was got up by six players. Cantona was suspended and threatened with the sack by the president Louis Nicollin.

It was during this year that Cantona reportedly underwent his speech therapy, attending a special school in Montpellier, it being thought that a tendency not to be able to finish sentences was causing frustration. He was deemed brave for his willingness to join under-16 pupils and use the Tomates method, which involved listening to reassuring tapes of his mother's voice.

He returned from suspension after a month, feeling that the air had been cleared, and indeed the team picked up. Cantona's form improved to the extent that he was swiftly brought back into the French team by Platini, with whom he was developing a promising relationship, and scored five goals in three matches. One of them was the winning goal against a German team who would go on that year to win the World Cup in Italy, but the highlight was a 4–2 win over an in-form Sweden. 'He told me before the match, "I am going to score two goals",' recalls Gérard Houllier, then Platini's assistant. 'And he did. And we were one down. He is that kind of fellow.'

The threat of relegation began to evaporate for Montpellier and the team set off on a Cup run. Cantona, linking well with the Colombian Carlos Valderrama, a gifted passer who could pick out his runs, scored a hat-trick in the round of the last 16 and another two in the quarter-final. They received a tough draw in the semi, away to St Etienne, but Cantona's neat volley took them to the Parc des Princes for a final against Matra Racing, who had beaten Marseille in the other semi. This was the crowning moment hitherto of Cantona's club career in France and his first senior honour. Montpellier won 2–1 and danced the night away on the Champs-Elysées.

They went into the European Cup-Winners' Cup, in which they would be eliminated by Manchester United, but without Cantona. He was now flavour of the month after his national team performances – he had scored nine goals in his last 11 appearances, including two in a 3–0 win over Scotland – along with the Cup win and 10 goals in 33 league matches. Tapie was being forced to bring back his *bête noir* from exile. Moreover, the coach now at Marseille was Franz Beckenbauer – who had joined in a coup that signalled Tapie's intention to win the European Cup, having just won the World Cup as coach to the Germans. Beckenbauer was also an admirer of Cantona. 'They had been forced to appreciate me,' Cantona said in his autobiography.

He was still reluctant, however. The autocratic Tapie touched a raw nerve with him, while the rebellious, turbulent Cantona upset Tapie. 'A personality clash' is the shorthand euphemism usually applied in the newspapers. Perhaps it was more that Tapie, with his financial power and charisma, was more used to yes-men, acolytes. Cantona saw himself as nobody's man but his own, one determined to be a free thinker and spirit. Stubborn, strong, like Tapie. 'Tapie did not like me but that was OK,' said Cantona. 'I, too, did not like him.'

By now Chris Waddle had joined the club. 'Eric started the season well, scored a few goals,' Waddle recalled to me. 'But I think a lot of fans were still disappointed with him, with the things he'd done before: the shirt-throwing and all that. They were very loyal fans, they worship the club and for them the shirt's everything. There were times when I thought, well, he's sort of playing and then a couple of games when he wasn't playing well. Then the crowd would get on his back and I just wondered is that because of what he'd done previously. When things weren't going well, his arms would go up and they didn't really like that. Personally, I got on OK with him. He used to come in in the morning and say, "Bonjour, ça va?", shake your hand, do a training session and go. He was quiet, yes, but I never had a problem with it. There never seemed to be any problem in training.

'Eric's got good technical ability. He enjoyed the training, and Beckenbauer was a big fan of his. I thought Eric was good as well. We played him and Jean-Pierre Papin up front, with me behind them or on the right side and someone on the left. Beckenbauer liked him to get in the box a lot. He used to let him just lay up and get in the box. Beckenbauer used him more as an

English centre-forward, to get him to try and come in at the far post, to use his head and his height.'

It went well. Cantona scored twice against Caen to begin a run of seven goals in his first 12 games. He also scored, along with Papin, for the national team in a 2–1 win over Iceland in Reykjavik in a European Championship qualifier. Gérard Houllier recalls the day. 'We were leading 2–0 about a quarter of an hour from the end and Michel took Eric off thinking that a more defensive player would help us keep the result. Eric went out of the ground and straight to the changing room. He got mad and furious, he was in a fit, and Michel and I realized something was wrong so we sent somebody to calm him down in the changing room. He did, and nobody heard of it. So Michel said to me, with a smile on his face, "I won't take him off again. He plays right to the end!"'

Then, in October, Cantona suffered a serious knee injury, damaged ligaments, in a tackle with Racine Kane of Brest. He would be out of action for three months. With Marseille not making the progress Tapie expected, Beckenbauer agreed, over the Christmas period, to a move sideways into an executive position, to be replaced as coach by the Belgian Raymond Goethals. It was also to spell the end for Cantona. 'I would never have any respect for Goethals because he never had any respect for his players,' was Cantona's opinion.

'By the time Eric was fit, we were playing well,' Waddle recalls. 'Abedi Pelé was playing up front with Papin, with me just behind, and Eric couldn't get back in the side. That's the way the system had developed from the 4–4–2 we had been playing when Eric was up front. Eric did like to drop off, to pass it, but we had a lot who could do that: Pelé, myself. Whenever players aren't in the side, and think they should be, they get cheesed off and it's very hard to accept. I don't think Eric and Goethals got on that well because of that, and Eric said: "Look, I don't want to be sitting around on the bench. I want to go and play in a side somewhere".'

He was playing in a side somewhere, and quite a side. Platini retained faith in him despite his lack of match practice (47 minutes in three months), and almost picked him for an international fixture in February 1991. Cantona did play in a 5–0 win over Albania at the Parc des Princes the following month.

The end was nigh at the Stade Vélodrome, however. Cantona was convinced that Tapie was pulling Goethals's strings and that he wanted him sold, the more so after Cantona had refused to back Tapie in a dispute over some derogatory remarks made by the president about the French Federation. In June Cantona was moving west again, this time about 60 miles, to another club with the grandiose 'Olympique' in their title. His 18 games played, with eight goals scored, during the season was enough to win him a first Championship medal as Marseille clinched the title. The move this time, though, was to altogether humbler surroundings, at Nîmes. The transfer fee was £1 million, less than half of what Tapie had paid for him.

As ever, Cantona arrived with a fanfare, and was even made captain of the club. When he played for France in a remarkable 2–1 win over Spain in Seville, where the host nation had not lost for more than sixty years, it seemed that this might be a new start, a brave new world. But the club reality was a disappointment, the team not up to the standard Cantona had hoped for, and he was to score only two goals in 18 matches. His frustration grew. 'The game wasn't giving me any pleasure and the spectacle that we were providing for the spectators wasn't very convincing. I did try very hard to be a good captain . . . the public was moaning, they were getting at me, the international who should have been able to transform things,' he was later to say.

Once more, frustration found manifestation. In December of 1991, Nîmes were playing St Etienne when Cantona took exception to a refereeing decision and threw the ball at the referee, hitting him on the legs. He did not even wait for the red card, exiting the pitch immediately. Cantona would soon be shown on *Les Guignols de L'Info* as a painter – painting himself a red card.

He was summoned to a disciplinary hearing. The commission decided on a suspension of four matches – not too bad, it seemed – but a tense meeting ensued as Cantona was given the verdict. What was then said, rather than the punishment, took Cantona over the edge. The president of the disciplinary commission,

Jacques Riolaci, said that they had received complaints from other clubs about his behaviour. Cantona replied that he should be considered only in the light of this one incident, and like any other player. 'You can't be judged like any other player,' said Riolaci. 'Behind you there is a trail of the smell of sulphur.'

Cantona's hackles rose. He got to his feet and moved to address each member of the commission in turn. 'Idiot,' he said to the face of each one. 'Remarkable restraint for me,' he would later say. The ban was extended to two months.

That was too much for Cantona to bear. On 12 December, 1991, at the age of 25, he announced that he would retire from football. For a month he walked on the beach at Grau du Roi in the Camargue, listened to music, painted – and missed football badly, mainly, according to him, its camaraderie. 'It's bizarre to be present at your own death,' he said. The Nîmes coach, Michel Mézy, who had shown considerable faith in Cantona, was beside himself, unable to get his star player to play. Mézy was left to rue: 'Eric is a bright, intelligent man who can become difficult to handle. This is his nature. When things go wrong, he does get upset. His temperament is fragile. But when things go right, then you can have nobody better in your team.'

In Paris, Platini and Houllier fretted. Their player, becoming so important to a resurgent national team, was in danger of slipping away from them. Houllier, an Anglophile who had been a language assistant in Liverpool in the early seventies and who was considered as Liverpool manager before Graeme Souness got the job, suggested to his colleague that England might be an option which would appeal to Cantona. It was one of the few countries in Europe where the transfer market remained open. A change of scene, one where the excesses of Eric Cantona were but curious newspaper paragraphs rather than headline news, might do the trick.

Platini travelled to Nîmes to see him. It did indeed appeal to Cantona: a chance to escape his situation and play football again, something for which he was pining. Platini, shrewdly, convinced him that his physique was well suited to the demands of the English game and that his technical skills would stand out. It worked.

To Michel Mézy's exasperation, he would lose his player but France would get theirs back. Cantona agreed to allow Platini, Houllier and Jean-Jacques Amorfini, vice-president of the French equivalent of the Professional Footballers' Association, to sound out opinion on the other side of the Channel.

Houllier, whose name was being mentioned in the summer of 1995 as a possible technical director for the English FA, has good contacts. He phoned Dennis Roach, upmarket English agent, formerly in the carpet business, for a quote. The man who brokered the Glenn Hoddle and Chris Waddle moves from Tottenham to Monaco and Marseille respectively, contacted Trevor Francis, then manager of Sheffield Wednesday but once a Roach client during his move as a player to Sampdoria of Genoa.

Francis phoned Waddle for an opinion of Cantona. 'I told him he was a good player but that it was a question of how he was handled,' Waddle remembers. 'I said his problem over here is that he flies off the handle at things. You just don't know if he's going to flare up. Talent-wise, I said he would do all right, but it was a risk.'

Cantona may have stumbled during his readings on the words in Rimbaud's *A Season in Hell*: 'Now I am accursed. I detest my native land.' Eric Cantona was ready for England, but was England ready for Eric Cantona, a character in search of an author?

'Just like an egg' was Guy Roux's verdict on the shaven-headed Cantona, here in action for the French Under-21 team. *(Onze-Mondial/Colorsport)*

Three days after describing the French national coach, Henri Michel, as a *sac à merde* and 'one of the world's most incompetent trainers', Cantona arrives at the French Football Federation to apologize. August, 1988. *(Popperfoto)*

'I did try very hard to be a good captain … ', but things didn't work out at Nîmes, Cantona's last French club. (*Empics*)

A rare performance in a Sheffield Wednesday shirt, against Baltimore Blast in an indoor friendly. Within a week he had moved on to Elland Road. *(Colorsport)*

Above An unmemorable performance in a dull match, but the home fans embrace Cantona after the final game of the Championship-winning season. *(Mark Leech)*

Left In discussion with Howard Wilkinson: during the summer of '92 Leeds' training was more geared to the passing game in which Cantona excels. *(Bedeau/Sport/Colorsport)*

Right With Cantona's hat-trick in the 4–3 Charity Shield win over Liverpool, Howard Wilkinson's dilemma about whether Leeds adapted to Cantona or vice versa appeared to have been solved. *(Mark Leech)*

Looks of love and disgust: Ferguson with his
favourite player *(Bob Thomas/Popperfoto)* and his
most troublesome charge. *(Colorsport)*

One for United's stamp collection: Cantona on Swindon's John Moncur. *(Colorsport)*

Old Trafford high point: after scoring against Arsenal. *(Colorsport)*

Highbury low point: an unlucky sending off at Arsenal. *(Colorsport)*

5   Yorkshire Bitter

Hello, I love you, won't you tell me your name?
Hello, I love you, let me jump in your game.
The Doors, 'Hello, I Love You'

It was certainly the most glamorous transfer negotiation that Graham Mackrell had ever negotiated, and he did not want it to end. In Paris at the headquarters of the Cacharel fashion house, the secretary of Sheffield Wednesday sat with Dennis Roach watching models in various states of undress coming and going between saunters down the catwalk while he waited to pursue his business with Eric Cantona and his representatives. Jean Bousquet, as well as being president of Nîmes Olympique football club, was also a big noise in Cacharel and had chosen the setting as convenient, even though a fashion show was going on that January day.

Roach had persuaded Trevor Francis that Cantona represented good business at £1.1 million, and Mackrell was despatched as envoy. In between the floor show, he spent three hours with Roach, Cantona, Bousquet and Jean-Jacques Amorfini of the French players' union. Eventually, it was agreed Cantona would leave the *haute couture* of Paris for the steel city of Sheffield.

Cantona arrived in England on 25 January, 1992, ready for a training session, a medical and what he thought would be the signing of contracts in Sheffield the following day. It was not to be that simple. With Cantona nothing ever has been, and there seemed no reason why it should be now. 'I don't think that was the case,' Mackrell told me. 'People like to rewrite history. My French is not that brilliant but I understood what was going on. We agreed that Eric would come over and see how things went, then take it from there.'

Wednesday were unwilling to commit themselves so swiftly to a player whose recent history showed that along with the talent came trouble. 'His c.v. showed that he did not stay anywhere too long,' says Mackrell. 'It was a club a season.' Francis's phone call to Chris Waddle's home in Aix-en-Provence had confirmed his own opinion that he needed to inspect the merchandise before purchasing, as well as his instinct to proceed cautiously before committing Wednesday's money. Francis, whose reputation as a man-manager has been questioned in the press after disagreements and reports of dressing-room unrest at both his previous club Queen's Park Rangers and Wednesday, told Cantona on his arrival that he would like to make a decision on him after a week's trial.

Cantona was miffed, his pride again dented. He had not been on trial since he was a teenager at Auxerre. He was by now a seasoned French international, who came with glowing references from Michel Platini and Gérard Houllier. Some players might have buckled down and determined to prove themselves to a new manager, but Cantona felt he had nothing to prove. With his sense of justice, and perhaps a little guilt that he had left them in the lurch, he also wanted Nîmes to receive back what they had paid Marseille for him.

He did decide to bite his tongue and stay for six days, training with the team and even making an appearance in an indoor friendly against Baltimore Blast at Sheffield Arena so that he could be introduced to the fans. 'From what I was told when I joined Wednesday, the lads said he did well,' says Chris Waddle, who returned to England from Marseille in 1993. 'But the grounds were hard and they had to train indoors a lot. He looked quite good though, they said, because his touch was so good.'

Snow and ice had come to Sheffield, and with outdoor training so limited Francis had not fully made up his mind. He asked

Cantona to extend the trial for a week. It was not about talent, says Mackrell; no one had really ever questioned that. 'It was more to see how he fitted in, how he got on with the other players.' But this Cantona could not take, and his lawyer Jean-Jacques Bertrand intervened on his behalf. Take it or leave it, Wednesday said, with sufficient numbers of strikers on their books anyway. Cantona, once again, was prepared to leave it.

'In hindsight, it looks a bad decision,' says Mackrell, who saw Francis leave the club in May 1995 after three seasons of much money being spent, a third place in the First Division and two Cup Finals having been reached, but with potential ultimately failing to be fulfilled. 'Many people have said that it was Trevor's big mistake, but I think that at the time it was the right decision,' Waddle agreed. 'A million pounds is still a lot of money,' he said. 'I would have done the same thing and Wednesday were flying at the time.' So too was Cantona – back to France.

It was clearly not to be a match, hinted at in a poem by Charles Baudelaire, appropriately entitled 'The Owls'. Perhaps it has since afforded Cantona himself a wry smile in his studies of the poet. He was not to take it to heart in his subsequent career in England, though:

> The wise man from their stance will learn
> In his short life on earth to spurn
> The vigorous and the turbulent;
>
> The men who passing shades embrace
> Will always bear the punishment
> For having wanted to change place.

At Elland Road, some 40 miles up from South Yorkshire, the Leeds United manager Howard Wilkinson had heard that Cantona was in England – just. Dennis Roach, perhaps beginning to worry that his commission from any transfer was going west, made sure that he did know. Wilkinson was on the look-out for a new striker as Leeds, becoming entangled in a Championship duel with Manchester United in only their second season back in the First

Division, had lost their leading striker Lee Chapman with a broken wrist sustained in an FA Cup tie against United.

Wilkinson, who had worked watching young players for consecutive England managers Ron Greenwood and Bobby Robson, remembered Cantona from an international Under-21 tournament in Toulon, and from the two-goal performance against England Under-21s at Highbury. He had, too, seen impressive snippets of tape. Lawrie McMenemy, then assistant manager of England, had also recommended Cantona after a conversation with Michel Platini. Wilkinson also sought opinions from Glenn Hoddle, by then the manager of Swindon and familiar with Cantona and French football from his time with Monaco, and Gérard Houllier, who returned his call from an airport lounge on his way home from an overseas tour with the veterans' team he plays for. He and Platini were now desperate to place their man; they would be unable to select him for the national team if he was not playing club football. Houllier spoke of Cantona's sense of justice, intelligence and loyalty. He also admitted he could be 'impulsive'.

While not desperate himself, Wilkinson needed to sign a striker to sustain the title challenge, to appear in control and to satisfy the fans. 'I had to take a gamble,' he admitted in his autobiography, *Managing to Succeed*, written with David Walker of the *Daily Mail*.

On that Friday, January 31, Cantona was preparing to leave the Swallow St George's Hotel in Sheffield – Wednesday grateful that they would not have to budget for his phone bill any more – and return to France, when a telephone call came that Wilkinson was on his way to speak to him. He chose to delay and would be glad he did. They talked, Cantona recalling it as being for one hour, Wilkinson as three or four. Cantona listened to tales of the thrills of English football, the atmosphere at Elland Road. Wilkinson said that he was interested only in what he could do for Leeds, rather than, as he called them, 'his goings-on'. Eventually Cantona was persuaded. 'I told him,' Wilkinson recalled to me when we spoke in his office at Elland Road, 'let's have a courtship. It might end in marriage or in Dear John . . .' Cantona was amused and was persuaded to accept a loan deal from Nîmes to Leeds until the end of the season. Leeds would pay an interim £100,000 and Cantona's wages with a view to a permanent transfer.

This was to be a marriage of opposites. Cantona, all the evidence said – and would do so again – was a wild and free spirit, capable of moments of sublime ingenuity and ridiculous banality; Wilkinson the archetypal Englishman was considered dour and wry. Those who attend his unsmiling, though thoughtful, press conferences may find it hard to believe that he once had an ambition to be a comedy writer, but his progress through the time-consuming business of football had precluded it. Formerly an English teacher, he was well respected in the game, having worked his way up through the regional coaching ranks to be manager of Notts County, Sheffield Wednesday and Leeds (he would also become the first president of the League Managers' Association). He was not, however, known to embrace such as the Gallic flair that Cantona might bring. Rather, his teams were solid of shape and organization, built on the work ethic. He had signed Vinny Jones from Wimbledon to help Leeds out of the Second Division. 'I firmly believe that for football success it is far more important to have character than to be a character,' was his basic footballing philosophy.

The following day Cantona sat in the stands as Leeds beat Notts County 3–0 at Elland Road, a result that confirmed them top of the table. Managers rarely enjoy the duty of the post-match press conference but this one Wilkinson relished, as he introduced his new signing to a stunned gathering. On the Monday Cantona reported for his first training session. 'His instinctive vision and instinctive passing skills were exquisite,' Wilkinson said in his autobiography. 'Eric lifted the proceedings to a higher level with a series of devastating flicks and passes.' Wilkinson also sensed the appreciation of the other players. 'Players are like animals,' he told me. 'They quickly recognize that there is a pecking order and are quick to make assessments. The higher up you go, the more experienced players can tell. It takes one to know one.' Would that regard, Wilkinson wondered in his book, also apply to Cantona's character?

'He never changed the whole time he was there,' Lee Chapman, who was to become the closest of the Leeds players to him, told me. 'He was always very quiet, he always arrived fairly late for training and he wouldn't say a word. He'd get changed, do his training, train well, get showered – spend an age in the showers, half an hour sometimes. He really had no conversation, or very little, with anybody. He was very insular and didn't really try to get involved. The language was obviously a problem for him, but I think he was just comfortable with his own company. When he first came, he was very eager to impress. I know he was.'

The first Saturday, Cantona, reluctant to leave the dressing room due to all the cameras, many from France, was made a substitute for the match at Oldham Athletic and appeared in the second half. He was unable to do anything about a 2–0 defeat, however, a surprising one that dropped Leeds to second behind Manchester United. But Cantona had played his first professional football for more than six weeks. He was then given a start, wearing the number nine shirt, the next week against Everton at Elland Road, but was not especially impressive in a 1–1 draw. Clearly the six-week lay-off had affected his fitness, even if Cantona at the time would not agree. The pace of the games, Wilkinson decided, was such that Cantona would have to bide his time and would go back to being a substitute.

Meanwhile, Cantona broke off from his Leeds duties to play for France against England at Wembley, Platini grateful to be in a position to pick him. But there, too, he was a disappointment, comfortably marked by a specialist in that, if little else, Martin Keown. Centre stage was instead conceded to Alan Shearer, who scored a goal on his international debut in the 2–0 win for the home nation.

The moment when Eric Cantona truly announced his presence in England came on 29 February in a home match against Luton. He was told the day before that he would again be a substitute and was, again, not best pleased. But when the Leeds left-back Tony Dorigo was injured in the first half, Wilkinson reorganized and Cantona was given his chance. After the break, he broke the deadlock 12 minutes into the second half and his joy was uncon- fined. 'I just remember the look on his face,' says Lee Chapman, who would go on and score the second goal in the 2–0 win. 'It was unbelievable. He shouted out to me, "Chappee," and threw his arms around me, he was so delighted. It meant such a lot to him to score that first goal in English football.'

Cantona was an overnight sensation. The Leeds fans, picking up a chant first accorded by Republic of Ireland followers to their centre-half Paul McGrath, sang 'Ooh-aah, Cantona', and he himself basked in the adulation. He attracted more media interest than any other player Wilkinson had worked with and journalists from all over Europe arrived to seek his views on art, philosophy and politics. 'A natural room-mate for David Batty, I thought immediately,' Wilkinson wrote; which may have been a little unfair on the young Yorkshireman who, since moving to Blackburn Rovers, has been known to bury his head in the *Chronicle of the Twentieth Century* on long coach trips to away matches. Instead, Chapman, having acquired a little French during a three-month spell with Niort, was billeted with him and took him under his wing; along with Gary McAllister, who often went out with them for meals. *La famille Cantona*, Isabelle and Raphaël having joined Eric, had by now moved into a modest, rented semi-detached near Roundhay Park, where father and son would enjoy kick-abouts. Seeking a substitute for grandmother Lucienne's creations, he frequented The Flying Pizza in Leeds, and also made the odd appearance at Mister Craig's pub.

Cantona had to endure the substitutes' bench for three more matches, until an abject 4–1 defeat at Queen's Park Rangers. The following week he was assigned the number three shirt for the home match against Wimbledon and partnered Chapman, scoring in a 5–1 win. It began a run of four matches in the side, but Leeds could only draw the next two, against Arsenal and West Ham.

Then, on the first Saturday in March, with the Championship contest becoming increasingly fraught, Leeds travelled to Manchester City. The day was sunny, the hopes high. Despite some patchy form of late, Leeds were still top of the table. The Leeds fans were in fine voice, unlike the team. The 4–0 defeat took the wind from their sails. Cantona was anonymous, something rarely associated with him – as one fan neatly put it: 'When you watched

Leeds, your eye was just drawn to Cantona,' – but he was not alone.

Soberly, Wilkinson contemplated the situation. He decided that Cantona was still floundering amid the pace and endeavour of the English game. He called a meeting of the players the following week to explain that he had decided to revert to the team that had taken Leeds to the top. Cantona would be a substitute, who would come on once the speed of the game had subsided and hopefully then hurt teams with his skill. Having seen Cantona sit impassively through the meeting, Wilkinson took him aside afterwards to explain the decision – something he does not usually do with players who are dropped – in the best French he could muster. Cantona was shocked and disappointed.

'We played a very direct sort of game and I was the target man,' says Chapman. 'The ball was played quite early up to me and people fed off me. Eric really prefers to play between the midfield and the forwards. But we didn't play like that, so he would tend to be overlooked all the time. Eric really came into his own when the pace of the game had cooled down a bit and there was lots of space developing. Then he would make contributions. The style we played tended not to show him in his best light. He just needed a bit of time to adjust to the English pace.'

Despite his chagrin, Cantona again knuckled down and the following Saturday, at Chelsea, he came on to score a spectacular goal, his third and final one of the season. Receiving the ball some 30 yards out, he lobbed it right-footed on the volley over Paul Elliott, then back on to his right foot with his left, also without it touching the ground, before driving home a half volley into the far corner of the net and running to the crowd to milk the applause. It was indeed memorable, though by then Leeds had the game won. The players had responded well to Wilkinson's clearing of the air and return to basics. That Saturday night they were back on top of the table.

The next week, Cantona was again handed the No. 12 shirt for Easter, traditionally the decisive time in English football, and on the Saturday Leeds prised a 0–0 draw out of Liverpool at Anfield. They slipped to second in the table but it was a point gained rather

than two lost, and on the Monday they regained the lead with a
2–0 win over Coventry City. Then United, who had disdained
two points in drawing 1–1 at Luton two days earlier, fell 2–1 to
Nottingham Forest. Two days later they would lose again, 1–0
at an already relegated West Ham, and suddenly Leeds could win
the title the following Sunday, against Sheffield United at Bramall
Lane. Duly they did, emerging victorious, 3–2, in a bizarre
comedy-of-errors match. United's 2–0 defeat at Liverpool later
that day, confirmed the issue. That night, Cantona went to
Chapman's house for the celebrations, TV cameras contriving a
jubilant scene out of the somewhat downbeat atmosphere following the draining effect of the day.

Cantona's role in the denouement had been peripheral but the
Elland Road crowd revered him nonetheless. On the final Saturday, with the ground *en fête*, he was given another start, in Gordon
Strachan's No. 7 shirt, against Norwich City. This was the day
of the Championship trophy being passed round and a 74-gun
salute fired, one shot for each league goal scored. Cantona was,
though, substituted in the second half after an unmemorable performance in a dull match, enlivened only by a virtuoso solo goal
from Rod Wallace which won the game and which Cantona must
have envied. The warmth of the crowd towards Cantona was still
remarkable. So too the feeling in the city that day. I remember
passing under a road bridge in a taxi on the way back to the station
and seeing the graffito: 'Merci, Eric.'

The team was feted at a Town Hall reception, with the players
confronted by a raucous throng packed into the square beneath
them. Cantona was persuaded to take the microphone and say a
few words. He raised his arms, applauded the crowd, and said: 'I
am very 'appy. Thank you very much.' Then he proved, in the
first of many examples to follow, his ability to dispense a pithy,
memorable phrase. 'Why I love you, I don't know why, but I
love you,' he said. The crowd roared. Another quote for the
Cantona collection, one that two Leeds fans in the music business
would turn into the lyric for a record which disappeared without
trace nationally but did quite well in Yorkshire.

Cantona was being perceived as the final ingredient that turned

Leeds into a Championship-winning team. In fact, he made only six starting appearances that season, a further nine as a substitute and only just qualified for a medal.

'I think Eric's contribution has been overrated, yes,' says Lee Chapman. 'He was cited as one of the reasons we won the Championship, but he only joined in January, half the season had already gone and we were still in a strong position at that time. When he started a game, he didn't really make much of a contribution because he hadn't adjusted to the pace. It was only really when he came on as a substitute in the later stages that he really contributed. I think they overestimated what he contributed, and that demeans what the rest of the players did. The players who were already there were really the reason why we won it. Of the goals that he scored, only the one against Luton was a decisive goal. We were already ahead when he scored the others.'

Nevertheless, Howard Wilkinson felt that Cantona had done enough to warrant making his signing permanent, and Nîmes received the balance of their 10 million Francs, about £1 million. Wilkinson continued to have reservations, though. Not the least was the worry that while overseas defenders and midfield players had done well in the English game, strikers were a different matter in the domestic hurly-burly. Space was limited with teams unwilling to concede it, defending as soon as possession was lost rather than funnelling back to allow teams to come at them. Another concern, though a minor one, was the amount of parking tickets Cantona was picking up.

But Wilkinson still felt the potential rewards exceeded the risk. If he could graft on some style to his side's steel, have someone to ease the creative load on the excellent Gary McAllister in midfield, then this team might develop into one capable of disturbing the best of Europe in the Champions' Cup the following season. Besides which, Cantona simply spiced the place up.

'In that respect, I think he has proved the most successful acquisition Leeds have ever made,' Wilkinson told David Walker for his book, written at the end of that season. 'Even with the obvious language difficulties, he has presented a refreshing new angle on Leeds United affairs. If you rated his popularity with the fans against the hours and minutes he has been out on that pitch, he must be the greatest hero the Leeds supporters have ever had.' This from the manager of a club that featured in its history John Charles, Jack Charlton, Billy Bremner and Johnny Giles.

There was a caveat: 'I hope my faith in his ability is justified and he produces star quality on the field, because without that he has nothing and I have even less . . . The big question now is whether he has the character and intelligence to adapt that ability. We still don't know but in that respect, the next season or so will be make-or-break for Eric.'

Cantona went off to the European Championship finals in Sweden a more settled man. He, along with the French team, flopped, however; though they were kept good company by Graham Taylor's England: both teams' travails were evident in a drab 0–0 draw in Malmo. Cantona and Jean-Pierre Papin could just not get going and the team from whom so much was expected, having won all their eight qualifying matches with Cantona rampant, limped home in similar fashion to England, an early exit following the group games. They lost to the eventual champions Denmark, while England were being defeated by Sweden in Gary Lineker's abbreviated last match. It was to be the end, too, for Michel Platini, who stood down to be replaced by Gérard Houllier. Cantona went on holiday to the French Alps to paint.

The experience clearly refreshed him for in his first match back with Leeds, the FA Charity Shield, he scored a hat-trick – two right-foot shots and a header – in a 4–3 win over Liverpool at Wembley. By its nature, the TCR (traditional curtain raiser), as it is known to rather bored football writers who prefer more competitive occasions, is a notoriously bad yardstick on which to base a season's preview, but Cantona's performance raised hope, expectations and excitement. It also convinced Wilkinson that Cantona and Chapman could play together up front. He felt easier in his dilemma about whether Leeds adapted to accommodate Cantona, or whether Cantona adapted to accommodate Leeds.

Training was more geared to the passing game in which Cantona might excel, with the emphasis less on the direct. Some players, including Chapman, had their doubts. Though when Leeds began the season – the Premier League now in being – with a 2–1 home win over Wimbledon and a 1–1 draw at Aston Villa, and Cantona a certain starter, it seemed that normal service would be resumed. A dreadful 4–1 defeat at Middlesbrough, who would be relegated that season, then seemed but a blip as a porous Tottenham Hotspur were beaten 5–0 at Elland Road. Monsieur Cantona scored another marvellous hat-trick, the third a wondrous volley, and the *Daily Mirror* trumpeted him as 'Eric Idol'. Two games later, after a 2–2 draw at Liverpool, where he received a stiff early challenge from Ronnie Whelan and was subdued, he scored another two to give Leeds a 2–0 lead at Oldham before the wheels came off and two late goals earned the home side a draw. The Middlesbrough match had not been a blip, after all. Leeds's away form was to become progressively worse through the season: a 2–0 defeat at Manchester United, following the Oldham match, was to be further proof.

It was scarcely any form with which to go into Europe. Leeds had been drawn against the German champions VfB Stuttgart, the first leg away from home. It was to be the beginning of the end of Eric Cantona's marriage to Leeds United.

Leeds held their own, and Stuttgart goalless, for the first half but fell behind after 62 minutes to a goal by Fritz Walter. Cantona was now feeling a twinge around his hamstring region and gestured towards the bench. He attempted to limp on, however, and six minutes after the goal, as Leeds were seeking to regroup and contain, he received possession wide on the left, looking up to play a crossfield ball. Wilkinson could see from the bench that Leeds were stretched. 'No, Eric, no,' he shouted. But Cantona had committed himself to the pass, which Stuttgart intercepted, then immediately broke forward to set up another goal for Walter; two in six minutes. 'Fucking hell, Eric,' Wilkinson shouted from the bench, just audible on the television coverage. Cantona was substituted.

'That was the big turning point,' Chapman recalled to me later. 'Eric should have kicked the ball out of play, with his injury. But that was typical of Eric, you know. Even though he was injured he tried to play the spectacular ball. It was a fairly crucial goal. Suddenly at 2–0, it's a big psychological disadvantage. I think that's when Howard started to realize.'

Stuttgart went on to make it 3–0 and it looked as if Leeds would fall at the first hurdle. They were to get lucky, however. A fortnight later, on a night of vivid intensity at Elland Road, Cantona seemed determined to make amends and show his ability at the top level of club competition. First he headed down for Gary Speed to score with a stunning volley, then hooked home a third himself between goals by Chapman. But Stuttgart had scored what seemed a decisive away goal, and despite winning 4–1 on the night Leeds were eliminated. Or were they? The following day, it was pointed out that a substitute used by Stuttgart was classed as an overseas player, meaning they had exceeded the quota by one, and Leeds had grounds for protest to UEFA, the European game's governing body. UEFA duly upheld it, Leeds were granted a replay, and on neutral territory in Barcelona's Nou Camp stadium, where fewer than 7000 people rattled around in the 120,000-seater, they prevailed 2–1. Cantona began the match but was replaced by Carl Shutt, who scored the winning goal.

In the second round, Leeds were drawn against Glasgow Rangers, with the first leg in Scotland. They made a remarkable start, silencing the rabid Ibrox crowd when Gary McAllister struck home a volley in the first minute. Rangers fought back to win, though, thanks to John Lukic punching the ball into his own net and Ally McCoist's poaching. Amid it all, Cantona complained to the bench of having received a bang on the head and was replaced by Rod Wallace. To Wilkinson's annoyance, Cantona made straight for the dressing room. 'I remembered how the old Marseille manager had warned me,' Wilkinson was later to say in an interview with John Sadler for the *Sun*. ' "Remember, when the sun is shining he plays, but in England it rains a lot." ' In Scotland that night, the storm clouds were gathering.

Wilkinson decided to drop Cantona for a match in London against Queen's Park Rangers three days later. On the morning of the match there was the usual run-out to rehearse set plays.

Those of the squad not in the team were expected to act as opposition and were handed red bibs by the coach Mick Hennigan; often the first notice they get they are not in the team. 'It really is terrible,' says Chapman. 'I don't agree with that side of Howard's management, but there again he's an excellent manager, he gets results, so who's to say he's wrong? But as a player, it's not very nice at all.' Cantona was duly handed the red bib. It was more like a red rag. 'Eric tried not to show anything but you could tell he was hurting,' Chapman recalls.

Practice over, Wilkinson twice attempted to speak to Cantona in the lobby of the team's hotel but was ignored. Cantona skipped the team's pre-match meal and stayed in the room he was sharing with Lee Chapman. When Chapman returned, he found Cantona in what he describes as 'loud and leery' clothing, in opposition to the team's match-day attire of collar and tie. The jacket was a bright purple, the trousers light coloured and the socks red. 'I knew the manager would take one look at it and go mad,' says Chapman, who told Cantona that a team meeting was about to start and that he ought to hurry up.

Cantona arrived ten minutes late, Wilkinson having waited for him. 'I knew there was going to be a confrontation about it now,' says Chapman. 'Howard just ripped him off in front of everyone. It was quite embarrassing because you felt for Eric. He wasn't dressed in the right clothes and that was it. He just sent him home. Sent him off, there and then. It's one of those things you don't really laugh about. You know it's serious and you can see both sides of the argument.'

Cantona was due to leave for France straight after the game. Wilkinson suggested that an earlier flight might be more appropriate. An immediate one, in fact. It would not be the first time that he would forcibly be urged to take off back to his homeland. 'His pride was hurt,' Wilkinson recalled to John Sadler. 'But when does pride become vanity? When does a strength become a weakness?' Wounded Cantona did leave, and spent the week in France, missing Leeds's Coca-Cola tie at Scunthorpe. Wilkinson, given Cantona's history, wondered if his player would return. He did, in time to be named as a substitute for a home match against

Coventry City. The atmosphere was not so much frosty as deep-frozen.

Wilkinson would give him another chance and named him in the side to face Rangers in the European Cup second-leg match the following Wednesday. Gérard Houllier travelled from Paris to check on the progress of Cantona at Leeds, concerned by reports he was getting. World Cup qualification was occupying him; France had begun the season scratchily – losing 2–0 in Bulgaria, beating Austria 2–0 at home (in which Cantona had scored the second) – and a match against Finland at the Parc des Princes was beckoning. Houllier met Wilkinson on the afternoon of the match and was taken through a videotape of the game at Ibrox. Wilkinson left the French manager in no doubt that he was unhappy with Cantona's contribution, especially the march straight to the dressing room. Houllier commented: 'This is not usual in England, but in France I have seen many players leave instead of feeling concerned with the thing, with the bench, encouraging the lads and so on. I think Howard was very cross with him. He thought it was not right.'

A few hours later, Cantona would play well enough and score five minutes from time, but it was for nought, as an early goal by Mark Hateley stretched Rangers' lead and another by McCoist confirmed Rangers' place in the inaugural league stage of the competition. Houllier recalls speaking that night with Andy Roxburgh, the Scotland manager, and Alex Ferguson. And with Jean-Jacques Amorfini. 'He told me there was a crisis and we had to do something,' says Houllier.

The next day, Houllier made a call to Ferguson on his carphone. 'I had read in the paper that Manchester United were looking for a centre-forward, and at that time they had made a bid for Alan Shearer and David Hirst. Alex was good and said he was interested. So I said this was not my business, this was not my concern. I was not an agent – he had to deal with Howard. You could say that I was concerned, that I . . . help is a weak word, but I help.' Canny Ferguson, though, would not make an immediate bid; the price might be too high. He would wait until matters had deteriorated a little.

They were soon to do so. The following Saturday's match against Manchester City would be Eric Cantona's last in a Leeds United shirt, although there would be a few more acrimonious weeks for him to endure at Elland Road.

When Cantona returned from France after the QPR episode, Wilkinson made efforts to talk through the situation with him. 'I even offered him the chance to pick the team himself,' Wilkinson told John Sadler. 'He said: "Oh no. That is your job. Leave anybody out but not me. I have to play."' Cantona apparently added that he was finding it difficult to play up front with Chapman, with everyone looking to set up Chapman as they had done for most of the previous season, rather than him. Wilkinson decided to give Cantona his head and Chapman was dropped for the trip to Maine Road on November 7. 'I'd had one of my best starts to a season for some time and I was left out. I'd been scoring regularly. I know I had no right to be left out,' Chapman told me. 'I was shocked when I found out why later, because I wouldn't be capable of doing something like that. But Eric is very single-minded and if he isn't in control of the situation, and if it isn't all revolving around Eric, then he finds it difficult to play second string. He's not what we would call a players' player. He has to do it by leading or orchestrating. I believe he would be capable of going to the manager like Howard said he did.'

Leeds, as they had done the season before, lost 4–0. This time, though, there was little constructive or galvanizing that came out. The previous defeat by City had raised the doubts in Wilkinson's mind; now they were shouts. He was worried, more worried than ever, about Cantona's temperament and ability to fit in with the group of players he had. The style had been modified in an attempt to integrate him but it had not worked. Leeds were suffering an identity crisis. 'I firmly believe that the reason we had such a poor season is that we tried to accommodate our play to fit Eric into the team, but it lessened our effectiveness,' says Chapman. 'That's why, in the end, we were almost threatened with relegation and needed points to stay up rather than win the Championship. It was all down to changing our style of play. I'm convinced of that.'

Training became tense, Cantona occasionally ignoring the instructions: driving the ball when asked to chip it, chipping it when asked to drive it, according to a source at the club. 'When there is a personal confrontation between a player and the manager, you don't really take sides,' says Chapman. 'Howard obviously couldn't let it go on for too long.' Did he ever have any indications of Cantona's petulance or suppressed anger? 'Yes, that dark side you almost felt in training, and although there was never really anything, you could tell he had the capacity, yes, definitely, in tackles. He didn't take kindly to criticism at any time, in training or in an ordinary match.'

The young Leeds striker Kevin Sharp had himself served an apprenticeship after Cantona at Auxerre, where 'he was talked about as a very dominating character on and off the field', and thus had some insight into the divergence of the two cultures and what Cantona was going through. He went even further than Chapman, telling Richard Williams for the *Independent on Sunday*: 'He's always had a mad head on him. There is always the odd dirty tackle. He can be a bit sly. You'd never get someone from England doing some of the things he does. That annoys some players.'

It was just as well in such an atmosphere that Cantona and Wilkinson were parted for a while. After the Manchester City match, Cantona was left out of the Leeds side for a Coca-Cola Cup tie at Watford, which Leeds lost 2–1, and the following weekend was free of Premier League fixtures because of World Cup qualifying matches. Cantona went to France for the match against Finland, which he helped them win 2–1. The endgame would be played out on his return, however.

On the day after his flight back from Paris, Cantona complained of an injury during training and departed. He knew he would be left out of the team for the following day's match against Arsenal at Elland Road, which Leeds won 3–0, and was not seen again that weekend. On the Monday morning, a fax came through to Howard Wilkinson. Jean-Jacques Bertrand was demanding a transfer for his client. Cantona followed it up with one of his own, which Wilkinson put in his safe. Later it was used as proof, when Cantona became angry that his request for a move emerged in the press. Cantona was especially concerned that Leeds fans, with whom he had developed such a rapport, did not think badly of him. Bertrand added that Cantona wished to go to either Manchester United, Arsenal or Liverpool.

Wilkinson spent the week agonizing. First he tried clubs in Italy, France and Spain but, he says, found no takers. 'When we decided to sell him there was a sense of real disappointment,' Wilkinson told John Sadler. 'Because, if things suited him, the boy could play. To be fair he could also be a nice bloke as well. A good trainer, keen, no trouble with alcohol, fit and a good athlete.' Wilkinson added to me: 'Exceptional player, exceptional talent. Probably one of the most gifted players I have ever worked with. No Pelé, no Maradona, no Platini, but a top-class player all the same.'

Chapman concurred that Cantona could be very pleasant. 'If journalists phoned and asked to do interviews with him I would negotiate deals. I would get money for him without even trying. I made him a bit of money and he gave me little presents. He knew I was into wine and he once gave me a bottle of Mouton Rothschild '81 which he'd had given to him.'

Later that week, Bill Fotherby, the Leeds managing director, was on the telephone to Manchester United's Martin Edwards. He wondered if the United full-back Denis Irwin might be for sale. No, Edwards replied. Sitting in the office was Alex Ferguson, now ready to make his move. He wrote down on a piece of paper 'Ask about Cantona'. Edwards did. Fotherby said he would get back to him.

Wilkinson agreed to the deal when asked by his MD, who was keen on it himself, keen to get the club's money back. Wilkinson may have been reluctant as a coach to let go a player who had scored 14 goals in 35 games, 11 from 20 that season, but as a manager he knew it was good business. Leeds were to get back the £1.1 million they had paid Nîmes, from whom Cantona had 'retired'. 'He had a history of pissing off from previous clubs when things didn't suit him,' Wilkinson said in the *Sun*. 'I could see Leeds being the latest in line. We would have been left without our player and without a penny . . . I said, "OK, let's do it."'

He rang Cantona at home, who readily agreed to talk to United. Leeds would release a statement that the parting was 'by mutual consent', the old footballing standby designed, supposedly, to avoid acrimony in the press. On Friday 26 November, 1992, Eric Cantona became a Manchester United player.

There was speculation as to the 'genuine' reasons behind the transfer and it was even suggested – scandalously and falsely – that Cantona was sleeping with other players' wives. One was later to receive an out-of-court settlement from a magazine that printed the allegation. It was, in reality, both simple and complicated. Wilkinson and Cantona marched to different drums: Cantona the boy on a motorcycle; Wilkinson more of a saloon-car man. To this day, bad blood exists between the two. The player felt that the manager forced him out of Elland Road; the manager that the player forced his hand.

In his autobiography, Cantona says that he had trouble 'decoding' Wilkinson's language. 'His comments were strange and rather incoherent, in my opinion,' he said. 'One moment he would tell me that he wants me to know that I owe everything to him, that I am only a Frenchman lost in the English League, and at other times he would say to me that without me the team is nothing and that I am the essential part.' He claims also to have been told by Leeds supporters that he overshadowed Wilkinson and believes that the manager has trouble in dealing with players whose personality is larger than his own. 'The curious thing is that it was not the only time that he had acted in such a way with players who were well-liked by the supporters. Vinny Jones and John Sheridan had both previously found themselves in the same uncomfortable position. It is clear from all this that he does not like strong personalities who have a rapport with the fans.'

Upon publication of the book, Wilkinson was stung into his interview with the *Sun*, the fee for which he asked to be donated to Leeds-based charities. 'Here was a player from whom I'd put up with tantrums, disappearances, sulks and an intolerance of being dropped,' he told the paper. 'I'd even taken him to one side and told him he was playing against Liverpool in the Charity Shield twenty-four hours before my other players knew the line-up. There have been times when I wish I had not bothered with him in the first place.'

The marriage had ended bitterly. And in a way, the wrangle was a microcosm of the English game. Cantona, the wayward magician, had brought some Gallic sleight-of-foot to the North of England; had provided a team possessing the basic Englishness of grit and graft with some new tricks. Wilkinson, the straight man, had attempted to weave some fantasy. But the two had not been compatible. The wand was now passed to Alex Ferguson.

6 La Vie en Rouge

If you tame me, then we shall need each other.
To me, you will be unique in all the world.
To you, I shall be unique in all the world.
Antoine de St-Exupéry, *The Little Prince*

The Manchester United players were attending a celebratory function being hosted by the city's Lord Mayor. All were in club
blazers, grey flannels, white shirts and official red and black ties.
Except one. 'What are you going to do about that, gaffer?' one
senior player asked of Alex Ferguson, pointing at this lofty figure
wearing some sort of tunic top and generally dressed for one of
the city's many trendy evening venues (Cantona has been known
to patronize the Hacienda club). Ferguson simply smiled.

It was an indication of two things: Cantona's need to express
his individuality, and the manager's willingness to accede to it.
Ferguson, a fiery but fair Scot with a reputation as a disciplinarian
every bit as tough as Howard Wilkinson's, dislikes the idea that
he treats Cantona with kid gloves – aptly demonstrated in his
bristling at questions as to whether any apprentice who did what
Cantona did would have been sacked. Clearly, he has indulged
him, however. 'The manager had to stretch a few principles
to accommodate a Frenchman who is his own man and who
obviously has had his problems conforming with certain

requirements,' David Meek wrote on Mark Hughes's behalf in the striker's autobiography, *Hughesie*. 'Alex Ferguson didn't exactly rewrite the rule book but he treated him differently and explained to the rest of us that he was a special player requiring special treatment.' For Ferguson is, too, a pragmatist and realized that if you were paying for a maverick talent, there was no point in shackling it. The other players may have had misgivings, but Ferguson believed that they, too, would come round if Cantona could add something to the team, could enhance their own status.

He had arrived at that approach after a study of Cantona's past, conversations with those who had known him well, like Gérard Houllier, and something that happened in Cantona's first league match for United (his debut was a midweek game in Lisbon against Benfica to celebrate the great Eusebio's fiftieth birthday). On 6 December United were playing Manchester City in an important derby. He was named a substitute but entered the fray at half-time with United a goal up. His first real contribution, after six minutes, was to pull wide to the right touchline, glance up and find Brian McClair inside the defenders Keith Curle and Terry Phelan with a reverse ball. 'That first pass was absolutely magnificent,' Ferguson was to say. 'Just the weight of it, the awareness of where the ball was going. It just encapsulated every-thing in him.' Moments later, Cantona's cross from the right wing was headed over by Mark Hughes.

It was promising material, even if Cantona himself did not agree. 'I played a mediocre game,' he said later, but Ferguson felt differently. His side beat City 2–1. Perhaps it was symbolic for Cantona, a turning point, after the two 4–0 defeats with Leeds United at Maine Road which had played such a large part in souring his embryonic career in England. 'In my first few matches, I was aware of coming to a club with a big tradition,' he said. 'I knew I had something to prove and that I had to earn my place in the side.'

An early training session also confirmed Ferguson's belief that at £1 million Eric Cantona was to be a steal. United's place of daily business, The Cliff, is in a leafy part of the Salford district of the city. It features just a small stand that has become familiar in film of the greats in training down the years, and which acts as minimal shelter from the worst excesses of the weather. It is a more welcoming place than many windswept venues next to motorways on the highways and byways of English football.

One morning at the end of a session, Cantona asked Ferguson if he could have the loan of two players. Ferguson wondered why but duly supplied two, plus a goalkeeper. Cantona proceeded to get in extra dribbling and shooting practice as Ferguson and his assistant Brian Kidd stood watching admiringly. 'I just said to Brian: "It's great management this. Fabulous. I just wish it was as easy as this all the time."' The other players got to hear and looked on. 'It's an amazing impact he has had on our club,' Ferguson added. He was also the fittest of players; tests showed that his body fat ratio was the lowest of all at Old Trafford.

Cantona got his first start the following Saturday at home to Norwich, replacing Bryan Robson, who was suffering from one of his regular injuries. He was not particularly impressive but did well enough in a 1–0 win that was United's fourth victory in a row and took them up to third place. The next Saturday, at Chelsea, he was off and running when he scored his first goal, a shot on the turn from close range that earned United a point. He had, after all, been bought for goals.

United had been suffering from a drought of them. It was as if Ferguson had learned from the previous season's failure to win the Championship, when the goals had dried up in midwinter: after a 6–3 win over Oldham Athletic on Boxing Day, they'd scored only 22 in their last 22 games; the first 20 had yielded 41. Had they splashed out on a striker that Christmas – say, an audacious bid for one last fling in the career of Gary Lineker, then with Tottenham Hotspur – the picture might have changed. Just when it seemed that they would win their first title for a quarter of a century, having led the table consistently in the first half of the season, they self-destructed and handed the title to Leeds.

The Sheffield Wednesday striker David Hirst had always been Ferguson's target, and it was even announced to a shareholders' meeting that a bid had been tabled, but injuries overcame him.

Ferguson took a £1 million chance on Dion Dublin from Cambridge United, but the striker broke a leg early in his United career. It seemed that Ferguson was fated not to find the player he wanted. United had slipped to tenth in the league by November 1992. Then came the day of the call from Bill Fotherby.

Howard Wilkinson had enjoyed 'unveiling' Cantona. Managers love to bask in the glow of signing a star and can barely resist announcing it from the top of the new stand. Lawrie McMenemy, when he signed Kevin Keegan for Southampton, told how he had had to bite his lip for a few days against all his own wishes; Terry Venables managed to be a television pundit during the 1986 World Cup in Mexico without letting on that he was signing Gary Lineker for Barcelona. The difference between men and boys, indeed, is just the size of their toys.

The day after Martin Edwards's phone call with Bill Fotherby, Ferguson was lunching with his then Manchester City counterpart Peter Reid and excused himself for a few moments to make a telephone call. When he came back, he confirmed to Reid the Cantona signing. 'He said to me, "Bugger off,"' Ferguson recalled with glee. 'I said, "Aye, it's right," and he said, "You've just made my week."'

The Championship had been United's grail for twenty-five years since Sir Matt Busby's heartwarming comeback from his injuries at Munich and his rebuilding of a team, a club. The magnificent team of George Best, Bobby Charlton and Denis Law had won the title in 1967 and gone on the next season to become the first English club to win the European Cup. Under such a shadow, Ferguson still lived; indeed Sir Matt still had an office down the corridor. Ferguson had endured a sticky patch after a couple of years at the club, which he joined in November 1987, but had turned matters around, winning the FA Cup in 1990 and going on to win the European Cup-Winners' Cup in 1991. They had also won the League Cup in the 1992–93 season. The title still remained the aim, though, with the European Cup to follow.

Ferguson hoped that Cantona might be the final piece of the jigsaw. He had assembled a formidable side: the Dane Peter Schmeichel was a towering last line of defence in goal; the back four of Paul Parker, Steve Bruce, Gary Pallister and Denis Irwin had been gradually, lovingly and expensively assembled. In midfield, Paul Ince had brought drive since his transfer from West Ham, with Bryan Robson, when fit, or Clayton Blackmore grafting alongside. On the wings, the prospects were exciting, with the Ukrainian Andrei Kanchelskis gradually coming to terms with the English game, Lee Sharpe bringing youthful dash, and the wonderkid Ryan Giggs becoming the first Ryan Giggs rather than the latest George Best. Up front was really the problem. The old questions about whether anyone could play alongside the robust Mark Hughes were surfacing. Brian McClair, who in 1987–88 – with Hughes then at Barcelona – had become the first United player since Best in 1967 to score 20 league goals in a season, was now less prolific.

English football was astounded by the signing of Cantona, with many commentators believing that Ferguson had made a grave error of judgement, largely due to the Frenchman's disciplinary record. The team that had collapsed in the title run-in was now looking for redemption to a player with a history himself of self-destructing. Cantona's move across the Pennines was certainly the most talked about mountain-crossing since Hannibal. Even the Manchester United players had reservations. 'I think everybody raised a few eyebrows, myself included, when the gaffer signed Eric,' the captain Steve Bruce was to say. 'Because I didn't really know about the ability he has. I had seen him at Leeds and knew he was a good player but I didn't realize the skills, the balance, the vision that he has got. As soon as I saw him in training, I knew he would give us another dimension.' It was echoed by Mark Hughes. 'Let's face it, Eric has had his moments,' he told David Meek. 'I must admit that at first I wondered whether it would end in tears with us as well, but it didn't take me long to take a different view.'

Indeed, Cantona's team-mates soon took to him. So too, did the United crowd. Old Trafford's noise can reach the level of a jumbo jet at full throttle, and amid it Cantona soon took off. The fans quickly adopted the 'Ooh-aah, Cantona' chant and would even enhance it by singing it to the Marseillaise. His imposing, imperious presence again drew the eye to him and the play, too, was similarly attracted to him, like a moth to a 100-watt bulb.

The burgeoning reputation was further enhanced on Boxing Day at Hillsborough, where he gave Sheffield Wednesday some evidence of what they had missed out on. It seemed Wednesday never had any need of him as they accumulated a 3–0 lead with 20 minutes left, the first goal being scored by David Hirst, and United's unbeaten run appeared at an end. Then Brian McClair pulled two back and finally Cantona struck. When a low cross came in from the left he was free at the far post but miskicked in attempting to sidefoot home. The Wednesday defence was wrongfooted, however, and he got a second chance. 'Maybe something was watching over me,' he was later to say.

'His arrival proved the missing link,' Mark Hughes was to tell Meek. 'The team felt right, balanced, and we were creating chances. The improvement up front also saw a tightening up at the back and confidence flooded through the team. Slowly but surely, the feeling gripped the team that no matter how a game seemed to be going against us, we were capable of pulling something out of the bag. We began to establish a reputation for not knowing when we were beaten.'

Now Cantona was a certain starter in the side, and four comfortable victories followed the Wednesday game: 5–0, 4–1 and 2–0 at home to Coventry City, Tottenham and Nottingham Forest respectively; 3–1 at Queen's Park Rangers. The drought was replaced with a deluge. Against Coventry, he felt confident enough of his place within the team dynamic to assume the role of penalty-taker, and in turn converted one. He felt confident enough in the dressing room, too, to offer to introduce his teammates to Rimbaud. 'Don't worry,' said one. 'I've already seen *Rambo I* and *II*.' In the Tottenham match, he opened the scoring with a looping header at the far post, and the reputation of only scoring goals with matches already won was beginning to detach itself. He also created the second goal for Denis Irwin. Taking a square pass from the left-back, he chipped a return into his path for Irwin to run on and shoot home. 'One of the passes of the season,' said John Motson for the BBC. It had illustrated

Cantona's ability to unlock a defence with a moment of ingenuity, a feat that had become rarer in the hurtling latter-day pace of top-level football in England. It was a moment of subtlety that seemed to make him, and United, that bit different from the bunch.

The fixture computer sent United to Leeds in early February and it was clearly going to be a difficult night for the team, and one man in particular. United's eleven-match unbeaten run in the league, from which they had gleaned 29 points, had ended with an unlikely defeat at struggling Ipswich, but they had rebounded with a 2–1 win over Sheffield United that took them back to the top of the table, Cantona scoring the winner after they had trailed 1–0. There is enmity between Leeds and United at the best of times. A section of the Elland Road crowd likes to sing an objectionable song that refers to the Munich air crash. I remember once on a train asking a Leeds fan with a Saturday evening sports paper how United had got on. He replied: 'Which one?' They detest Old Trafford's assumption that there's only one United.

The tension on Cantona's face was clearly visible as he danced from foot to foot waiting to kick off. It was a poisonous atmosphere. Hell hath no fury like a football crowd scorned. '*Foutre le Camp*' read one Leeds banner, an only mildly nasty phrase meaning something like 'Naff Off'. 'Who needs Cantona?' they chanted.

'It was tense, very tense,' Cantona was to recall. 'Some people thought of me as an enemy and treated me like a traitor. They called me every name under the sun. But what shocked me was the hatred of the fans. Between players things can get tense because we play to win, but there is no hate. But when you see Leeds fans making aeroplanes in memory of the crash of '58 it really shocks you. I'd been in England for a year and never seen such cruelty. When I saw that, the hatred towards me seemed less important. I put the game back in perspective. Not another word could touch me.' It was a far *cri de coeur* from the statements he had uttered about how wonderful the crowds were in England. He now saw the other side.

Every touch was jeered; when he chipped a chance wide, trying to score a clever goal that might silence them, the stadium erupted in howls of derision. Cantona looked hurt and baffled. There was delight when he was given the yellow card by the referee Kelvin Morton for elbowing John Newsome in the chest, retaliation for a push. Then, as Cantona sought the relief of the dressing room after a goalless draw, which while leaving a sour taste had at least not seen any excess, he was involved in an incident near the players' tunnel.

Some Leeds fans claimed that Cantona had spat at them. He asserted that he spat at a wall. It was left to an FA disciplinary commission to determine the truth. The next month they decided to punish him with a £1000 fine after finding him guilty of misconduct. They conceded, though, that there was mitigation in 'the provocation he was subject to prior to the incident'. It was a minor forewarning of events to come. Cantona claimed that Steve Bruce had been spat at earlier; if so, here was an example of him retaliating to the treatment of a team-mate with his singular sense of justice. This would happen again. At the same time Cantona also received a two-match suspension for passing twenty-one disciplinary points, most of them accrued during his time at Leeds. More than a year in England and his first suspension. Not bad.

After the fixture at Leeds, Cantona returned to France to play in a World Cup qualifying match against Israel in Tel Aviv, scoring the first goal in a 4–0 win. He missed United's FA Cup fifth-round tie at Sheffield United. They lost 2–1. The now regular penalty-taker absent, Steve Bruce hit a post with one.

He was back, though, the following weekend and helped United to a 2–1 win at Southampton in the first of three important league wins for United. A 3–0 win over Middlesbrough, in which Cantona scored the third, was followed by a rare 2–1 win over Liverpool at Anfield, the scene of their final-hurdle fall the previous season. It took them back to the top of the table and was the more satisfying having been achieved without Cantona, who was serving the first game of his two-match suspension. They lost the other, 1–0 at Oldham.

Cantona returned in mid-March against Aston Villa, at Old Trafford. United were locked in a tussle for the leadership with a Villa side managed by Ron Atkinson, Ferguson's predecessor at Old Trafford. A titanic struggle ensued. Steve Staunton gave Villa the lead with a marvellous left-footed cross shot but Cantona, heading back a cross from the left-wing, laid on an equalizer for Hughes.

They had at least avoided defeat, as they did against Manchester City in the next match when Cantona delightfully glanced home Lee Sharpe's cross for the goal in another 1–1 draw, but United were now wobbling a little, which was confirmed in a tough goalless draw at home to Arsenal. They had now slipped to second, behind the surprise package of the season, Norwich City, who the same day had beaten Villa 1–0. United's next game was at Carrow Road and would be central to determining the destination of the title. If they lost to a side playing bright passing football under their progressive manager Mike Walker, United would be four points adrift and memories of the previous season's travails might well return to haunt them.

On a spring Monday night in East Anglia, United managed to play with a freedom that belied any such thoughts. 'We played a perfect game,' Cantona was to say. They were, indeed, initially unstoppable and raced into a 3–0 lead after only 21 minutes. First Cantona sent Giggs racing clear, then Kanchelskis further exploited a square Norwich defence on the counter. Finally, Ince burst through and found Cantona in space on the right for a simple sidefoot home. It all illustrated his versatility as both creator and finisher. Norwich reduced the deficit in the second half but United were not going to let this slip. The East Anglian side had been neat enough, and passed the ball as well as the pretenders to the Championship, but in Cantona United had a player with something they lacked; a player with a bit of devil in him – red devil.

The match engendered new confidence in United, though there was still the traditionally tricky Easter period to negotiate. Sheffield Wednesday, having recovered from a bad start to the season to become FA Cup Finalists, were the visitors to a nervous Old Trafford on the Saturday and took the lead with a penalty by John Sheridan. Deep into the second half, the referee pulled a calf muscle and was replaced by a linesman. To this day, Chris

Waddle, playing in that match for Wednesday, believes that the linesman forgot to start his watch until seven minutes had passed. 'I think we got robbed,' Waddle says. 'Where did he get seven minutes' injury time from? We couldn't work it out. Even if he'd played two minutes, that would have been over the top. There were no injuries. There was nothing.'

Whatever. In added time, with United laying siege to the Wednesday goal, Steve Bruce scored twice with headers to provoke Alex Ferguson and Brian Kidd into scenes of clenched-fist celebration at the sideline, Kidd even going down on his knees in gratitude just on the pitch. United had eked out a fortunate win. Cantona had been denied the possession he needed to hurt the opposition due to Sheridan and Waddle's ability to retain the ball for long periods. His and United's rhythm had left them. But their luck had turned, it seemed, with Villa being held 1–1 at home by Coventry, to whom United were to travel on the Monday, to leave United a point clear at the top.

The Wednesday match was also notable for Cantona having to depart the action with a broken right wrist, to be replaced by Bryan Robson. Ferguson was in two minds about whether to start him against Coventry two days later but Robson magnanimously stepped aside. The team was settled and playing well, he said. A goal by Denis Irwin brought a 1–0 win, Cantona contributing despite his bandaged hand.

The previous season Howard Wilkinson had pointed out during the run-in, when Manchester United were slipping, that teams need to accumulate points in anticipation of a wobble that will inevitably come. It was not to arrive for United this time. The following Saturday Chelsea were well beaten 3–0 at Old Trafford, with Cantona gilding the lily in scoring the third goal. Four days later came a 2–0 win at Selhurst Park, Cantona supplying the cross for Hughes to volley home the first goal. It was a joyous night at a stadium that would come to contain nothing but bitter recollections for Cantona. Four wins in a row had turned up the heat to a level that saw United's rivals boil over. Against such middling sides as Chelsea and Crystal Palace, Cantona's ability to dictate the pace and pattern of the game had been decisive. No midfield player picked him up consistently, no defender was willing to be drawn out from the back line.

Cantona, himself, went off to experience warmth of another sort. A difficult World Cup qualifier against Sweden was in the offing. After 15 minutes, he was later to say, he was sweating profusely due to the clamminess of a spring Parisian night and the intensity of the match. He remained cool enough, however, to convert a penalty and then, in the 85th minute, add the goal that saw France to a 2–1 win and on course for the following summer's World Cup in the United States. It may well have been his best game for his country: he seized control of it. He was a success abroad and now felt as big a player as any in France, ranking with Jean-Pierre Papin, Marcel Desailly and David Ginola. All seemed well enough in his own world.

It got better. On Sunday 2 May Aston Villa lost their penultimate game, 1–0 at home to an Oldham Athletic side fighting for their Premier League lives. Suddenly United were champions. Alex Ferguson heard the news on a golf course; Eric Cantona while lying on his bed in his Manchester hotel room. The telephone rang; it was Steve Bruce inviting him to a party at his home in Bramhall. Cantona arrived to hear the Queen song 'We are the Champions' blaring out.

The following night for the final home match, against Blackburn Rovers, Old Trafford was raucous with relief and celebration. The crowd went through its repertoire of songs: 'Simply the Best', 'We are the Champions', 'Always Look on the Bright Side of Life'. And of course, for the benefit of their messiah and the amusement of Michel Platini, Gérard Houllier, Jean-Jacques Amorfini and Jean-Jacques Bertrand, all sitting in the stands, 'Ooh-aah, Cantona' to the Marseillaise.

Blackburn took an early lead through Kevin Gallacher but United were not to be denied a sixth consecutive win (a last-day 2–1 success at Wimbledon would make it seven) and responded with goals by Giggs, Ince – supplied by Cantona – and Pallister, the one player bar Schmeichel who had not previously scored that season. Cantona also desperately tried to lay on a goal for Bryan Robson. The garish new Premier League trophy was jointly held aloft by Bruce and Robson, but the lasting memory was of the venerable Sir Matt Busby, beaming proudly. The long wait since his own team's Championship was over.

Cantona had clearly made the difference, as Ferguson was to acknowledge. 'Without question, he was the catalyst in us winning the Championship,' he said, choosing the right word: the dictionary defines catalyst as an agent that effects chemical change in other bodies. 'We had some tremendous young players just emerging and Eric came at the right time for them. He brought the sense of big-time thinking, the vision and imagination and general play. Players like Paul Ince, Lee Sharpe and Andrei Kanchelskis all responded.' 'Cantona is someone you want on your team,' Ince told Jim White for his book *Are you Watching, Liverpool?* 'The very fact he's playing, his presence on the field, his awareness of where everyone is on the field, it sets you up. You want that beside you. He can take it all in straightaway, what's happening. Whereas it takes me two or three seconds to work out who's where, he knows it straightaway and he can pick them out, in the right positions, at the right time. Cantona, man. Respect. Bona fide respect.'

He had indeed turned United from a side capable of challenging for the title to the winners of it. Leeds had already been well set, and set in their ways. Howard Wilkinson's attempts to develop them more into a passing team were in their infancy and required more than one player. United, preferring open, ground-based football, had accommodated him with comfort, nurtured his talents and he in turn nurtured theirs.

Cantona had finally found the right position for himself, aided by an open-minded Ferguson, who had also solved the problem of a partner for Hughes. By playing Cantona a little withdrawn from the central striker, 'in the hole' as the professional terminology has it, United had surprised many teams, who became uncertain whom to depute to counter; midfield player or defender. From there, Cantona could instigate attacks with his roving eye and arrive late in the penalty area to finish moves. Other players in the English game had toyed with the position and it was scarcely anything new. Indeed, Glenn Hoddle had deemed it his best pos-

ition in his Tottenham days. But few had played it with such
authority. On the continent, in France, it was a *de rigueur* tactic
but the English game was often still set in its rigid formations.
Such flexibility, if given its head, as Ferguson did, could bring
the new dimension. Hughes liked room to breathe up front, time
to hold the ball up and spread it. Cantona was never in his way,
never running on too soon.

'An artist has no homeland,' wrote Alfred de Musset but, outside of his, Cantona had finally found a home. Old Trafford can
make players, but it has also broken many, especially strikers.
Peter Davenport, bought from Nottingham Forest, springs to
mind; Alan Brazil used to be physically sick in the dressing room
before games, so onerous did he perceive the responsibility of
scoring goals for Manchester United to be. Cantona had quickly
settled as if to the manner born. 'Eric just swaggered in, stuck
out his chest and looked around,' said Ferguson. 'He surveyed
everything as though he were asking: "I'm Cantona, how big are
you? Are you big enough for me?"'

He was now big back home again. Cantona celebrated that
summer, before a holiday in Budapest to visit brother Joël, who
was then playing for Ferencváros, by accepting an invitation to
take to the catwalk for a Paco Rabanne fashion show in Paris, his
strutting hauteur made for the *haute couture* medium. From such
a setting, he had left for Sheffield Wednesday, and now returned
to his country a success, with two Championship medals. Having
scored nine goals in 22 appearances for United, and having played
on a losing side just once, he was also able to thumb his nose at
all the doubters. To boot, there had been no real reappearance of
the dark side of his nature. Headlines about *Le Brat* were long
forgotten.

A blip on this healthy cardiograph came at the start of the 1993–
94 season, which United began by winning the Charity Shield
against Arsenal, 5–4 on penalties (Cantona scoring one of them),
when he suffered a knee injury and was forced to miss the start
of the campaign. International duty, when he played in a satisfying
1–1 draw for France against Sweden, extended his absence to four
matches. By now United had the swagger of aristocrats about

them, however, and won three and drew the other of those four to assume the leadership. Cantona marked his return at Southampton with a splendidly chipped goal 20 yards out on the left edge of the penalty area to set up a 3–1 win. Ferguson turned to Ryan Giggs, sat alongside him on the bench, and said: 'When you reach that level of accuracy, you can call yourself a player. You're watching a master at work.'

That autumn, United's football was the best the top flight in England had seen for a long time. Roy Keane had come from Nottingham Forest for £3.75 million to lend heavyweight support to Paul Ince in midfield. Now the team was complete. Kanchelskis and Giggs provided breathtaking dash down the flanks; Cantona dropping deep to play off Hughes, was both talisman and touchstone. Like a quality control supervisor, all things went through him.

The next match was exhibition stuff, a 3–0 win over West Ham with Cantona backheeling and chipping away delightfully. A 1–0 defeat at Chelsea the following week, when Cantona almost scored an outrageous goal, his lob from 45 yards bouncing on to the bar, simply stirred them into a run of eight wins in a row. Against Arsenal, Cantona scored with a piledriving shot from 25 yards to break the deadlock in an epic clash of England's heavyweights played at an astonishing pace; these were the velociraptors of the game.

A large dark cloud was to appear on their horizon, however. United had been drawn against the Turkish champions Galatasaray in the European Cup; a formality before taking a place in the league stages of the competition, it seemed. That feeling had grown up from United's performance in the first round against Kispest Honvéd, once one of Europe's great names but now fallen on hard times. Cantona had scored the third goal in a 3–2 victory in Budapest, a narrow margin that barely reflected their superiority, and the second leg was won 2–1. Another untroubled passage seemed assured when United soon took a 2–0 lead in the home leg against Galatasaray. The Turks stunned Old Trafford, though, by recovering to lead 3–2. It took a goal by Cantona in the dying minutes for United to retain any hopes for the second leg in Istanbul.

United were billeted in a former Sultan's palace overlooking the Bosporus, Cantona appearing on the balcony almost papally for photographers. He could also be snapped playing chess with his room-mate Peter Schmeichel. It was a peaceful scene at odds with others being played out around them – in which Cantona would ultimately become entangled. 'Welcome to the Hell' and 'Welcome, Mr Cantona. After the match you say, Goodbye, Mrs Cantona' read banners being displayed by a noisy crowd at Istanbul airport on their arrival; though the show was largely orchestrated by Turkish television. Ferguson was asked at a press conference about the 'riot'. 'That was a riot, was it lads?' he wondered. 'You've obviously never seen a Glasgow wedding.'

On the night itself, the Ali Sami Yen Stadium was a hostile inferno and United seemed intimidated. So, too, their support, though many of them had not made it, having felt the full, arbitrary force of the Turkish police, pulling them from their beds the night before the match and holding them during it. As for the game, Ferguson, with problems over which of his 'foreign players' to leave out, opted to omit Mark Hughes. Stripped of his striking partner in a match United had to win to progress, Cantona grew more and more frustrated. He is no leader of a line; rather a player who feeds off one. Ferguson elected to flood the midfield with Bryan Robson, Paul Ince and Roy Keane and hope that one moment of inspiration from Cantona could bring the win needed, but he was crowded out when he sought to drop off deeper from the defence. The spearhead Cantona needed was missing. When Denis Irwin was heavily tackled near the touchline late in the game, and the ball ran on to a cinder track, Cantona charged over to retrieve it, aware that time was running out. There he sought to prise the ball with his foot from a Galatasaray official who was trying to hold on to it. A mêlée developed but order was restored.

Until the final whistle, that was. Cantona moved towards the referee, Kurt Röthlisberger of Switzerland, and joined thumb and forefinger of his right hand to form a circle, indicating, he claimed, that the referee had not played any stoppage time. Alternatively it could have been the zero mark he believed the referee merited for his handling of the match. Röthlisberger interpreted it as dissent and a derogatory gesture and showed the red card. As Cantona left the field, a fracas developed between United players and Turkish police as they exited down steps to a tunnel that led to the dressing rooms. Cantona claimed to have been hit by a baton. Bryan Robson's hand was gashed and needed stitches.

Afterwards Cantona gave another of his emotional heat-of-the-moment interviews that had seen him banned in France following his comments about Henri Michel. He had also, a few weeks before Istanbul, announced that, after France had damagingly lost a home World Cup qualifier 3–2 to Israel, he would not play again for the national team in the Parc des Princes while it was only half full. Now he said to French journalists that the referee must have been bribed. Later, Cantona was banned from European competition for four matches, the comments clearly not helping. With United out of the competition, it would not matter. This season, at least.

On the following Sunday, United clearly had a hangover as they fell 2–0 behind at Maine Road to City. But after half-time they regrouped, and Cantona seized the moment. First he pounced on a mistake by Michel Vonk to pull back a goal, then turned home a low cross by Giggs for the equalizer. Finally, Roy Keane completed a remarkable recovery.

More disappointment for Cantona in international competition followed ten days later, however, when France sensationally lost their final World Cup qualifier 2–1 to Bulgaria with all but the last kick of the match. Having seemed strong for so long in the group, they would not now be going to the United States. Sweden and Bulgaria, both of whom would go on to reach the semi-finals, had nosed ahead of them.

There were huge recriminations in France, not least among the players. Cantona blamed David Ginola, the Paris St Germain striker, for the mistake that led to Bulgaria's winning goal. Ginola would not accept it. The game should have been taken to the provinces, the players said, as the Parisian crowd were a muted, cynical bunch. Indeed they were. The French public, expecting great things from a talented team, were left deflated and heard little about the players accepting responsibility themselves.

French international football had been a laughing stock for many years after failing to build on the 1958 team of Raymond Kopa and Just Fontaine, which finished third in the World Cup in Sweden. Qualification for any major tournament was a struggle usually beyond them until the once-in-a-generation Michel Platini arrived on the scene in the late seventies. Then Jean Tigana and Alain Giresse joined him in the exciting side that reached the 1982 World Cup semi-finals and thrillingly won the 1984 European Championship. Cantona and the new breed were to be their heirs, messengers of a new golden era.

The 1992 European Championship finals had shown that perhaps hopes were too high, but when the French public switched on their Sunday night football programme, *L'Équipe de Dimanche*, and saw Cantona delighting Old Trafford, Jean-Pierre Papin and Marcel Desailly taking their places in the magnificent Milan team, it was little wonder. The disappointment was bitter and the scepticism that had developed around the national team in the dark days of the sixties and early seventies returned. On the day following an exciting stage of the Tour de France or a successful night for a French club side in European football, the circulation of *L'Équipe* often doubles from its usual 300,000. Since the Bulgaria match, it does not change if the national team wins, loses or draws.

The players, it was felt, were nothing more than overpaid egomaniacs, and it was true that there was a clash of egos between Cantona and Ginola, each probably a little jealous of the other. Cantona had made good as one of the legends of world football; Ginola was the pin-up Parisian. Playing them both in the same team was an exercise in optimism. Ginola's move to Newcastle United in the summer of 1995, taking a pay cut to £15,000 a week in the process, was probably influenced by what Cantona had achieved and a desire to emulate his success. Perhaps – or to his alarm perhaps not – Newcastle would build around him as United had with Cantona. Paris St Germain, with such a virtuoso as the Liberian George Weah, since sold to Milan, had been reluctant to do so, and Ginola felt slighted. In turn, Cantona felt himself a star when he returned to France and possibly some of the modesty, humility and respect he demonstrated to team-mates at Old

Trafford deserted him when placed in the national team, where he was still allowed to play in the hole behind Papin but was expected to work harder, deeper. In that may have been a reason why England was now his haven.

But back in a domestic environment, Cantona excelled anew. He headed the winning goal at Coventry, streaked through for a goal in a 3–0 win over Sheffield United and, on the anniversary of his first goal for the club, scored twice against Aston Villa in a 3–1 win, holding off the considerable presence of Paul McGrath for the second. At the half-way point of the season, United were 13 points clear of their nearest challengers Blackburn Rovers, with whom they eked out a 1–1 draw at Old Trafford thanks to Paul Ince's late equalizer. Another 0–0 draw at home to his *bêtes blanches* Leeds United was followed by the match of the season, against Liverpool. Within 20 minutes, an irresistible United were 3–0 up, Cantona crossing for Bruce to head home the first, Giggs chipping a marvellous second and Irwin curling home a free kick for an even better third. Liverpool then responded spiritedly and eventually claimed a 3–3 draw. That first half hour, though, was a remarkable exhibition by United. No longer did they fear Anfield – in fact they feared nothing. Cantona had no baggage of failure or inferiority to bring with him, as did United when it came to Liverpool, and his attitude of arrogance on the field was clearly communicating itself to the other players. United were now the first violins.

January witnessed a sad moment in the history of Manchester United with the death of Sir Matt Busby, aged 84. The Saturday following, United were playing Everton at Old Trafford. To be there that day was to witness the most moving of occasions. Outside the ground, hundreds of floral tributes were laid beneath the Munich memorial; inside there was the most reverential of silences while a bagpiper playing 'A Scottish Soldier' led out the teams. Fittingly, United gave a vintage display of attacking football. A goal by Giggs was scant reward; Cantona deserved another for one moment of supreme skill, bringing a cross down on his chest, swivelling in one movement and volleying against a post. Sir Matt would have much admired this, as he much admired Cantona the player. It was probably for the best that he was not around to see the events of Selhurst Park.

Neither would he have cared very much for something that happened eight days later. United were setting out on a new FA Cup campaign and in the third round had again been drawn against Sheffield United. This time Cantona was available and with him they had avenged their defeat of the previous season, winning 1–0. It sent them to Norwich for the fourth round and the temperamental side of Cantona, along with his poor tackling technique, came to light. Feeling that the normally mild-mannered Jeremy Goss had come in at him with studs showing, Cantona pursued Goss, now in possession, and, from behind, aimed one foot at his calves and wrapped the other round his shins. It earned him a lenient yellow card, fortunate not to be turned to red when he later sank his studs into a prostrate John Polston's shoulder as the two became entangled. He was thus on the field to score United's first goal, unlocking a tight match, which they were to win 2–0. Jimmy Hill, analysing the match for BBC's live coverage, described Cantona's behaviour as 'despicable'. Alex Ferguson responded when told of Hill's comments: 'If there's a prat going about in this world, then he's the prat.' He added: 'Eric probably reacted to a bit of off-the-ball intimidation. He knows he doesn't have to get involved in things like that. You can't take the law into your own hands, but at least some of his passing was incredible.'

In a more rational moment, though, Ferguson did acknowledge a deficiency in Cantona. 'He's not a tackler,' the manager admitted. 'I have told him: "Don't bother tackling, because you can't." I am fed up telling him. When he gets into tackles he doesn't know how to do it, so he ends up getting a booking. I don't think forwards are expected to tackle abroad, you see. You don't see them haring about tackling centre-halves. They conserve themselves for the things that are more important: scoring and creating.' Rather than simply executing a mistimed tackle, though, the Goss incident was clearly an example of Cantona, with his sometimes misguided sense of justice, exacting retribution.

In the next round, a different side of Cantona would surface. At Wimbledon he was subjected to a lunge, as bad as the one on Goss, by a Vinny Jones clearly attempting to undermine his effectiveness early in the game. He just walked away, however, and went on to score one of his most memorable goals for United. Gary Elkins could only head a clearance to Cantona, some 20 yards out to the right of the home side's goal. He cushioned the ball with his right foot, then sent a searing volley beyond Hans Segers into the far corner of the net. United went on to win 3–0 and in the next round would beat Charlton Athletic 3–1 to reach the semi-finals.

In the league, Blackburn had made a spirited charge at United's lead and a 2–0 win over Liverpool, on the day United lost 1–0 to Chelsea for the second time in a season, cut the deficit to four points. Matters were becoming tense now this fevered March, the only respite being a 5–0 win over Sheffield Wednesday in which Cantona scored twice. He and United had overcome the problems Wednesday had set the previous season, pressing them out of possession, not allowing them to settle. Then, physically more dominant, technique took over. In many ways this mixture of physique and finesse that United had become was that of Cantona himself. But it could be difficult to balance the two sometimes, as the events of a match against the hapless bottom club Swindon Town at their humble County Ground were to prove. There, tension turned into turbulence.

Feelings ran high from early in the game, when Mark Hughes was punched by a spectator as he sought to collect the ball for a throw-in. It passed almost unnoticed by commentators, but not by the United players. Then, midway through the second half, Cantona tangled with the Swindon midfield player John Moncur and spitefully stamped on his stomach as he lay at his feet. Duly, Cantona was shown the red card and United went on to squander two points in a 2–2 draw. Jimmy Hill would have been justified, too, in describing this Cantona action as despicable. 'If he played for Wimbledon,' said the Swindon player Lawrie Sanchez, who had been schooled there and should have known, 'he would be sent off every week. He is full of niggles and nastiness. He's your typical Gallic.' Moncur said he would still vote for Cantona as his Player of the Year.

Four days later at Highbury, Cantona was in more trouble though this was less deserved. He was correctly given a yellow card for a rash tackle on Arsenal's Ian Selley, but when he was dismissed after colliding with Tony Adams – both players with one eye on pursuing the ball, the other on each other's bulk – an injustice appeared to have been done. The crowd and officials were treated to a defiant fuck-you stride to the dressing rooms, but later even some Arsenal players spoke out on his behalf.

It cut little ice with the authorities, though, and Cantona was suspended for five matches; probably what he deserved from the Moncur incident. Other treatment was less justified. One tabloid headline, 'Mad Eric Brings the Nightmare Back', was bad enough but now he was being pursued by news reporters desperate for tittle-tattle about the dark side of this man who had previously brought light. Cantona recalls being tailed in his car for signs of him having some affair, and of being offered a cigarette so that he could be morally condemned for smoking. *L'Équipe* ran a headline '*L'Angleterre Contre Cantona*'. For the first time since he had joined United there were fears that he might regress to his old behaviour when the going got tough. The United captain Steve Bruce confessed to being worried that he 'might just pack it all in'.

In the meantime, there was a Coca-Cola Cup Final against Aston Villa at Wembley to contest, United's astonishing season having seen them dispose of Stoke City, Leicester City, Everton, Portsmouth and Sheffield Wednesday. Mad March continued, however, and they were comfortably beaten 3–1 by the underdogs in a tactical triumph over his old club by Ron Atkinson. He pulled Dalian Atkinson wide to disrupt United's normally solid back four and the central striker responded with a goal in the 3–1 win. Cantona was largely anonymous. There would be no treble.

Respite came in a tetchy 1–0 win over Liverpool in the last match before Cantona's suspension, which then began badly at Old Trafford with two splendid goals by Alan Shearer – one thumped home, one headed firmly – giving Blackburn Rovers a 2–0 win. The gap was now only three points.

It was clearly a struggle without Cantona. They were still the more than competent side who had finished runners-up before his arrival, but they simply did not possess the same awesome aura. They looked mortal again. In the semi-final at Wembley, United fell behind to a goal by Oldham's Trevor Pointon. United's season was again in danger of imminent collapse until Mark Hughes popped up in the game's dying breath to guide home a remarkable volley. With Andrei Kanchelskis fit to bring renewed vigour as compensation for Cantona's continued absence, United breezed through the replay 4–1. The relief was tempered by Blackburn beating Villa 1–0 and drawing level with United on 79 points, though having played a game more. At Old Trafford a narrow 3–2 league win over Oldham was followed by a 1–0 defeat at Wimbledon and, now United's hopes of retaining the title, once a foregone conclusion, had been eroded.

Cometh the hour, cometh the banned man. Cantona's impact on his return was immediate and decisive. It would ease all the tension, so apparent in the disciplinary misdemeanours and in Ferguson's comments of the time, created by observers wondering if he had lost his grip on the club and his players.

It was the return derby of the season but Manchester City were no longer the scourge of Cantona; indeed the opposite was the case and they were duly put to the sword at Old Trafford. Thanks to Kanchelskis's spade work, Cantona had a tap-in for the first. His second, to bring a 2–0 win, was precisely taken. Goalkeepers are taught to 'stay big' when confronted by an attacker running through at them, in other words to delay committing themselves to inspire doubt in his mind. Andy Dibble did just such but Cantona had another way to skin the cat, cutely slipping it under him with no backlift to his right foot. It was an example of his technique and improvisational ability. United were now back on track and four days later another English ghost was laid for him. This time he enjoyed a return to Leeds, with United winning a huge victory 2–0 thanks to goals by Kanchelskis and Giggs. Blackburn were finding it hard to live with the pace and failed to beat Queen's Park Rangers at home.

'That was the turning point,' Cantona said later of the following, scrappy, 2–1 win at Ipswich, in which he scored the first goal, heading an equalizer as United struggled against a team desperate to avoid relegation. 'The main thing is to keep control and win,' he offered by way of explanation. 'It can't always be euphoria.' Now United were five points clear with two matches to play. Finally Blackburn cracked, losing 2–1 at Coventry. United celebrated their second successive title with a 2–0 win over Southampton, their fourth consecutive win since Cantona's return.

The Cup Final beckoned, against Chelsea, the only team to have beaten them twice that season, and with it came the opportunity to perform English football's classic Double. Only three teams this century had done it – Tottenham, Arsenal and Liverpool – along with Preston North End in the less competitive times of the last. Alex Ferguson had already achieved it in Scotland with Aberdeen.

Chelsea were the less nervous, more lively team in the first half and came close to scoring when Peacock, scorer of the goals in the two 1–0 league victories, hit the bar. After the break the game turned. Eddie Newton brought down Irwin, and Cantona, not enjoying one of his best days, stepped up and coolly stroked the penalty to the goalkeeper's left as Dmitri Kharine dived right. Soon after, Kanchelskis tangled with Frank Sinclair and a more contentious penalty was awarded. Cantona duly replicated his first kick and the game was over. Even below par, he could still galvanize others by his presence, reassure the team and give them a sense of superiority. Goals by Hughes and McClair brought United a deserved but flattering win at 4–0.

Cantona had talked of the penalty kick in his autobiography. 'The penalty kick is the most fearsome of actions, but it is easy to execute. I enjoy this moment that holds all those who are watching in suspense. It's terrible, with the executioner face to face with his victim. Fifteen seconds punctuated by a flash of lightning. The crowd explodes or crumbles. The penalty is either happiness or sadness, nothing else.'

United had done the Double and had deserved to; their party, for which the players dressed in Blues Brothers outfits – black suits, hats and sunglasses – was well merited. This was a team which had dominated the English game with a breathtaking brand of fluent football; Cantona's role crucial with his capacity for the unexpected and the brilliant. His striking ability alone had brought him 25 goals from 48 appearances. Eighteen had been scored in the league. United had lost only two matches in which he was playing.

Of course, there was the crass, which surfaced when United's tension, and possibly that of their volatile manager, was at its height. Cantona's role in that, too, was central, threatening to undermine the magnificent structure. Of the three league games he had been suspended for, United had lost two of them. His return merely emphasized how important, almost indispensable, he had become.

Cantona had been the first Frenchman to play in an FA Cup final and now he became the first foreign player to be voted Player of the Year by his fellow professionals. The votes had been cast before the Moncur incident at Swindon, but he would probably have still received them anyway. He failed to win the Football Writers' Award, which went to Alan Shearer instead. That honour calls more for fair play and co-operation with the press. Cantona, at times, had displayed neither.

He resisted the temptation to turn up at the PFA dinner in jeans, instead conforming to the dress code of dinner jacket and bow tie, his slicked-back hair giving him the air of a Latin lounge lizard. His speech was charming. Accepting the trophy from Terry Venables he said: 'I am very happy and very proud to get this prize tonight. I would like to say first I owe my success to Manchester United, to my manager Alex Ferguson, my coach Brian Kidd, all my team-mates, the staff, the fans. After that I would like to congratulate other people from football in England, even the players who didn't vote for me, for the pleasure they give me to play in this magnificent football, English football.'

That summer, Cantona did get to go to the World Cup in the United States. The US is one of his favourite countries – for its vastness and variety – despite the commercialism he has said he detests. French television had hired him as an analyst, yet here, still, controversy courted him. And not because of the 200,000 Francs he was receiving from France 2, which upset some back home still annoyed that he was not there as a player. Attempting to gain entry to the commentary position for a match at the Rose

Bowl in Pasadena he was involved in an altercation with a security guard. It was minor stuff but indicative of the trouble that follows Cantona even to places where he is little known. I had considerable sympathy for him this time. The security was indeed ludicrous at the venue: for the third-place match between Sweden and Bulgaria, journalists had to queue for thirty minutes to get into the press box while FBI officers conducted personal searches, even taking out batteries from computers.

Another harbinger of anxiety was glimpsed in a pre-season tournament in Glasgow during a match against Rangers, in which Cantona challenged the host club's defender Steve Pressley with his studs showing. His dismissal cost him a three-match suspension that precluded him from United's opening to the Premiership. United covered for his absence well enough, beating Queen's Park Rangers and Tottenham and drawing with the exciting newcomers to the division, Nottingham Forest. Cantona's return, in which he scored in a 3–0 win over Wimbledon, suggested that domestically United would be as formidable as before. The European Cup was the priority this season, however, as diversionary league defeats in September and October to Leeds, in which Cantona's penalty was but consolation, Ipswich and Sheffield Wednesday appeared to confirm. There was also a defeat at Newcastle in the Coca-Cola Cup, with all but a reserve team.

This time United were seeded straight through to the Champions' League, being drawn against Barcelona, IFK Gothenburg – and Galatasaray. Initially all seemed well, despite Cantona beginning the four-match suspension carried over from Turkey, when Gothenburg were beaten 4–2 at Old Trafford. He was not required to make the trip for the Return to Hell, the match in Istanbul, as his presence might have seemed provocative. United were happy enough this time with a 0–0 draw, which was now worth one point, and for once the talk was of someone other than Cantona. The high profile Ryan Giggs, following his modelling appearances and the publication of the ridiculously early *My Story*, was struggling to make an impact. Why had the wonderkid not yet turned into superman? A bout of tonsillitis and an ankle injury offered two reasons.

That September, England were playing the United States at Wembley and their coach, Bora Milutinovic, was asked which English players he admired. 'Cantona,' he replied. Pelé would later say something similar when asked to comment on the state of the English game. They might, though, have thought differently had they consulted the French press after a match that month against Slovakia. Cantona had by now been made captain of the national team by Aimé Jacquet, and had begun in Japan in the Kirin Cup. On the day before the Slovakia match he unilaterally refused to speak to French journalists, telling them to get off the team's back. His tactics were not redeemed by his and the team's performance as they struggled to a 0–0 draw.

Domestically, things went smoothly. By now he was more settled, having moved the family from an unpretentious semi in Leeds to an unpretentious semi in the Boothstown area of Greater Manchester. Son Raphaël, pestering Dad for a Peter Schmeichel haircut, would perhaps now grow up with a Lancashire accent instead of the Yorkshire one he was acquiring. Eric, meanwhile, drove in his grey Audi 100 to enjoy the odd hour at the Bridgewater Hotel pub in nearby Worsley over a fruit juice or Pernod ('*le vrai pastis de Marseille*').

At Old Trafford Cantona scored the only goal in a victory over West Ham and added another in an epic 4–2 win at Ewood Park. It was, however, a somewhat fortuitous victory over a team who were destined, again, to be United's strongest challengers. With Blackburn leading 2–1 referee Gerald Ashby sent off the home right-back Henning Berg after a tussle with Lee Sharpe, awarding a penalty at the same time. Cantona converted for an equalizer. It came in an intense period of the season for United. In the next league match they gave what was to be one of their best performances of the season, defeating Newcastle 2–0 and ending their opponents' exciting, eleven-match unbeaten start. This was a display more in keeping with the previous season.

In between, though, there was a glimpse of trouble ahead, with a 2–2 draw against Barcelona at Old Trafford. United, salvaging a point with a late goal, a clever backheel by Lee Sharpe, were tactically and technically in the Spaniards' wake. They were duly cut adrift in the return in the Nou Camp stadium a fortnight later as the Brazilian Romario and the Bulgarian Hristo Stoichkov sent them to a 4–0 defeat. Amid the cacophony of 110,000 home fans the suspended Cantona sat impassively, wearing baseball cap, alongside Schmeichel, left out for the English goalkeeper Gary Walsh so that Ferguson could select three overseas outfield players. At least Cantona would return, his ban completed, for the match in Gothenburg three weeks later.

After three impressive league victories – 2–1 at Aston Villa, 5–0 in the Manchester derby and 3–0 at home to Crystal Palace, Cantona scoring in the latter two – hopes were high for the trip to Sweden. A draw there and an avenging victory over Galatasaray a fortnight later should have seen United through to the quarter-finals. So much for the theory; it became a huge deflation for United with Cantona and co. overwhelmed. Nervous, they began by unintentionally playing an unfamiliar offside trap and were soon punished. After that Ince and McClair in midfield could assert no authority nor supply Cantona, floundering amid an atmosphere with which he had been unacquainted for more than a year, with any quality of possession. Kanchelskis did not involve himself sufficiently. After conceding an early goal to the bright young left winger Jesper Blomqvist, Cantona fashioned an equalizer for Hughes only for the side to lose concentration and another goal soon after. Gothenburg eventually ran out comfortable 3–1 winners, the ignominy compounded by Ince's sending off. Ferguson's quest to emulate Sir Matt Busby was put on hold.

The inquests began. United did not have enough English players, being forced to shuffle the pack continually between Europe and home; the sometimes knockabout nature of the English game was scant preparation for the technocracy of European football; Cantona's absence, through his own fault, for so long had cost them dear. And when he did play, were the suggestions that he may not be a player for the biggest of club occasions, as Howard Wilkinson indicated at Leeds, really true? A 4–0 win over Galatasaray, in which Cantona saw a group of young English players through against accommodating, already-eliminated opposition, only added to the debate and the sense of what might have been. He had brought such young talents as Simon Davies and David Beckham into the game with some searching early passes, but also received a yellow card to follow one in Gothenburg. Had United somehow qualified – Gothenburg winning in Barcelona instead of drawing – Cantona would have missed the first match of the quarter-finals.

United now had to set about domestic matters with new vigour and Blackburn were proving tough nuts this season. A 2–1 home defeat by Nottingham Forest, Stan Collymore in exceptional form, scoring a marvellous goal with a swerving left-footed shot to upstage Cantona's goal, emphasized United's task. Otherwise, Cantona was keeping them in contention, scoring in wins over Norwich, Chelsea and Coventry, the latter a penalty. Once again the third round of the FA Cup sent them to Sheffield United, and Cantona's temperament was tested again – and almost found wanting. The combative Sheffield midfield player Charlie Hartfield was at Cantona's heels early on, and the Frenchman responded with a sly kick as Hartfield ran into a mêlée following a foul on a United player. Who knows, had Cantona been shown the red card here, Selhurst Park in sixteen days' time might never have happened. But the rod was spared and the child was spoiled. Hartfield was instead sent off for clutching Cantona's throat in a bout of retaliation. Cantona stayed on to score a superb chipped goal off the underside of the bar in a 2–0 win.

Ironically, I was at Crystal Palace's training ground the following morning to put together a feature for the *Independent on Sunday*. The manager Alan Smith was conducting a soul-searching team meeting. 'Look at Manchester United last night,' he said. 'They seemed to know they were going to win that match. They have a belief in themselves, and we've got to find that.' A player piped up. 'They've also got a Cantona,' he said. 'We haven't.'

They also had a new signing, one that, like Cantona's in midseason before, took the football world by surprise. To bolster Blackburn Kenny Dalglish had signed Chris Sutton from Norwich City the previous summer for £5 million. Ferguson needed a response. His was to go and buy Andy Cole for a British transfer record of £6 million plus the talented winger Keith Gillespie. Ferguson had wanted Stan Collymore but the Forest manager Frank Clark refused to take his calls, claiming illness. Perhaps remembering his audacious signing of Cantona, Ferguson instead phoned Kevin Keegan at Newcastle, more in hope than expectation. He was surprised and delighted when Keegan accepted the offer.

Cantona, it seemed, would have a new partner up front. Mark Hughes would consequently be sold, probably to Everton. Reluctantly, with European competition in mind, United had decided to transfer the Welshman so as to create a vacancy on their roster for another English player. Hughes would play his final game against Newcastle; a rider to the deal being that Cole would not play in the forthcoming match between the two clubs at St James' Park. As one might have expected in such circumstances, Hughes duly scored to give United the lead, bravely turning home Cantona's headed flick, but in doing so gashed a knee in a collision with the Newcastle goalkeeper Pavel Srnicek. Newcastle later equalized and Cantona missed a good chance to win the game when his volley drifted agonizingly wide of the far post. The headlines were thus about Hughes. He would be out of action for a few weeks and Everton's bid was in abeyance.

Meanwhile, Cantona was training with Cole, seeking out the livewire striker with through passes in training. A marvellous double-page picture in *L'Équipe* magazine at the time had Cantona in possession running forward, head up, eyes as alert as a bird of prey. Around him, their own eyes on the ball, faces a study of concern, were the players providing opposition in training: Denis Irwin, Gary Pallister and Lee Sharpe. Ahead of him, his eyes also on the ball and ready to make a run when the pass was released, was Cole. Cantona was looking into the space ahead of Cole.

The pair would start their first match together at Old Trafford, in a crucial top-of-the-table encounter against Blackburn Rovers, who were five points clear. It would be the only one they would finish together. Cole missed a good early chance to open his account but Cantona's brilliant headed goal, on the run from Giggs's cross, stole the points. A headed 'goal' by Tim Sherwood in the dying seconds was ruled out for a push on Keane by Alan Shearer discerned by the referee Paul Durkin.

Cantona's goal was invaluable, pegging Blackburn back to a manageable distance when they might have been further towards the horizon. But it was to be only a legacy. It was Cantona's last goal of the season. Selhurst Park came three days later. The two teams had been evenly matched. Both played the game with ferocious pace and commitment, both were of a solid 4–4–2 shape. There had been only one difference, only one decisive moment, only one man . . .

Ferguson's call for the team to respond positively to life after Cantona produced the 5–2 win over Wrexham in the FA Cup and a 1–0 victory over Aston Villa. That day Cole scored his first goal to extract United from a hole, and the following week he was prominent as they cruised to a 3–0 victory in the Manchester derby at Maine Road. 'Three-nil without Cantona,' sang the United faithful, dotted around the stadium in between odd bouts of fisticuffs. Clearly the segregation had gone awry and the taunts were, in hindsight, provocative and an omen. Still, but for a hiccup at Everton, revitalized by new manager Joe Royle, they piled on the wins, including one by an astonishing 9–0 over Ipswich in which Cole scored five. His freshness was compensating; Cantona was barely missed, it seemed.

'But I think that Eric's influence was still there in that he gave them a sense of confidence and assurance to go all the way. I think he raised their game,' says David Meek. 'Mark Hughes said that he taught them a little bit of European football. The example he gave was that he taught them the importance of what looks at first sight to be a negative pass: I pass it to you, you pass it to me, and nothing's changed on our side. But the pattern of play goes on, the opposition has moved, and there's a better angle to pass. The crowd may not have appreciated that sort of passing, which looks as if it's for the sake of passing, but Mark said that they played like that even without Eric, and it improved the team play.'

There was, too, another FA Cup run: wins over Leeds and Queen's Park Rangers taking them to a semi-final. Against Crystal Palace. What goes around comes around. All this was being played out against a backdrop of Cantona's various hearings – not to mention Paul Ince's – before the FA and Croydon magistrates court. Occasionally Cantona would slip into Old Trafford to watch games, but his being there only emphasized how much – for all United's attempts to cover up – they were beginning to miss him: notably in goalless draws against Tottenham and Leeds, when a moment of his ingenuity might have turned one point into three, and in what looked like a crucial defeat at Liverpool. Blackburn now enjoyed the sort of lead United had the previous season. Astonishingly, however, United rallied themselves with five successive wins to take the title race to the final day, Blackburn having limped to the line following defeats by Manchester City and West Ham. Remarkably, United had the title in their own hands for a few minutes on the final day while Blackburn were losing at Liverpool. Then Andy Cole failed to take one of two tricky late chances in a siege on the West Ham defence at Upton Park, and a 1–1 draw saw them fail by a single point.

Cantona, meanwhile, was in France that day, playing in a charity match for the Varieties Club de France celebrity team, a 2–2 draw against an amateur team, Marly-le-Roi. It annoyed the FA but Cantona had permission from FIFA. 'Playing again for me is fantastic, and to do so for a humanitarian cause is even better,' he said.

The Cup semi-final against Palace was to prove a symbolic, almost shambolic affair. Even in his absence Cantona's presence hung over the event, with a fan being killed as a result of a pre-match fracas. It would figure prominently when it later came to discussion about whether Cantona could remain in England.

The Final against Everton illustrated it again. Without him, United had little subtlety or ability to unlock a resolute defence and fell to a 1–0 defeat. A week earlier, repeating the Double had been a possibility; no team in England had ever done that. Now both elements were gone. And Cantona had missed 29 games through suspension, 22 of them as a result of Selhurst Park. 'It changed the life of Manchester United,' Ferguson was to reflect. He also described it as seeming like an 'enormous curse on us that will never go away'. Eric Cantona, who had given Manchester United everything they craved, had now cost them everything. At a huge personal cost, too.

7 The Marquis de Sardines

See these eyes so red
Red like jungle burning bright
Those who feel me near
Pull the blinds and change their minds
David Bowie, 'Cat People'

Eric Cantona might have known he was in for another bout of
ridicule when his taxi brought him to the four-star Croydon Park
Hotel just before dawn on Thursday 23 March, 1995. Hoardings
in the satellite town on the London–Surrey border – called the
capital's Manhattan for its skyline developed during the high-rise
days of the sixties – were advertising an exhibition locally of the
work of Picasso.

Cantona and Paul Ince were due to appear at Croydon magistrates court in a few hours' time, both on charges of common
assault resulting from the night at Selhurst Park. This particular
night they had chosen to spend in rather more entertaining circumstances; for them, if not the media. After United's 3–0 win over
Arsenal at Old Trafford, Ince drove to join Cantona for a night
in the West End of London. Until 2.30 a.m. they patronized
Brown's in Covent Garden, a haunt of pop and rock stars and
models such as Naomi Campbell and the INXS singer Michael
Hutchence. Then it was on to the Emporium club in Kingly Street,

which sounds like a gentlemen's club, but is more for blokes. There, the artist formerly known as Prince was giving the second of two private concerts. Cantona and Ince enjoyed the company of a new slimline Paul Gascoigne, the artist formerly known as fatty, and the film star Mel Gibson, until 4.50 a.m.

If Cantona was feeling somewhat short of sleep, he was to be rudely awoken by his day in court. It should have been a simple, ordinary case, one that courts deal with routinely and several times every day in every small town in England. It was, *bien sur*, neither simple nor ordinary. For a start, the gathering of evidence had occupied ten officers of the Metropolitan Police. So many were needed because there were so many witnesses to interview, they claimed. Normally such a case diverts only one from more serious inquiries. A murder investigation in south London running simultaneously was occupying six officers.

It was a sunny spring morning as Cantona, escorted by the now ubiquitous United security man Ned Kelly – how the club must have been wishing he had been pitchside that winter's night a few miles away – ran the gauntlet of photographers and curious bystanders lining the 100-yard walk from his hotel to the magistrates court.

Out of superstition, Ince was normally last out of the Old Trafford dressing room before a match, putting on his shirt only as he ran on to the field. Today he was first into Court One, shirt already donned. As he was pleading not guilty – to Cantona's guilty – the case would take longer than his team-mate's so he was given unconditional bail until a trial date in May. Then he stayed on to hear the Cantona case; if you had a seat it was a shame not to. Less flippantly, Cantona must have felt somewhat lonely amid such a gathering, and a familiar face might help.

The prosecutor, Mr Jeffrey McCann, first reminded the court of the events of 25 January: Cantona's sending-off, his walk along the touchline, Matthew Simmons leaving his seat and moving eleven rows to the front to harangue Cantona, who responded with his kick to the chest of Simmons. 'Cantona fell back, got on to his feet and went to strike Simmons with his fist, it seems, two or three times,' Mr McCann continued. Actually, it was only once. 'Simmons defended himself by punching back. At that point Cantona was restrained by officials and led off the pitch.' He added that it was only good policing and stewarding that prevented the episode from escalating into 'a major public disorder'.

It was here, he said, that there was a difference in the accounts of what had been said by Simmons, who himself was facing a court appearance charged with threatening behaviour. One witness, who described himself as attending that night as a neutral, said that Simmons had shouted: 'You fucking cheating French cunt. Fuck off back to France, you motherfucker. French bastard. Wanker.' The magistrates' clerk, Mr John Manning, broke in at this point. 'Can you follow what is being said to you, Mr Cantona?' he asked. 'Yes,' said Mr Cantona. The court, tense and looking for release – as was Cantona – broke into laughter. The player would hardly have taken such serious umbrage that night had he not understood, would he? It emerged that Simmons himself had told police he had shouted: 'Off, off, off. Go on, Cantona, have an early shower.'

The evidence relating to Simmons was clearly unsound, Mr McCann agreed. The prosecutor offered to show the court videotape of the night's events but the chairman of Croydon magistrates, Mrs Jean Pearch, said the court did not need to see it. They had to have been on Mars not to have done so already.

The court did hear Cantona's statement, read out by his barrister, Mr David Poole. This was Cantona's first and only account of the night. 'Shortly after half-time, I was dismissed from the field for an offence against an opponent. I was angry and frustrated with myself at my dismissal but did not protest to the referee,' it said. 'In my opinion, his decision was correct, although I had been repeatedly and painfully fouled in the course of the match.' No mention here of the anger at the treatment of Andy Cole that Cantona's mother had spoken of.

It went on: 'As I was leaving the field and making my way towards the players' tunnel I was deeply disappointed with myself for what had happened. I then became aware of a man to my right near the front of the spectators' terraces, one of a number who seemed to be shouting and gesticulating at me. At first I could not hear what he was saying, but it was very soon clear that he was goading and taunting me because of my sending off. His face appeared to be contorted with hatred or rage and he was making an obscene gesture. He was shouting in abusive, insulting and racist or nationalistic terms.' No mention, either of the reference to his mother that had apparently so upset him. 'I was obviously hurt and insulted and, with the addition of this to my existing frustration, I reacted in a way I now deeply regret: by jumping up and kicking out towards the man's chest. I am very aware that I should not have done this and I am not seeking to justify this. At this stage, I fell over. As I got up, the man swung his fist at me, once, and I swung my fist once at him. I was then led away.' He also denied reports that he had broken appointments with South Norwood police. That might have been so: he could have gone to Guadeloupe before there was chance to make any.

Mr Poole made a spirited defence of his client, sometimes a 'volatile and tempestuous footballer', he conceded. Of the confrontation, he said, 'One of them had been hell bent on trouble, and that man was not Mr Cantona.' Simmons, he said, 'was one of that regrettable minority who put xenophobia before any love of soccer, and express that xenophobia, which footballers who are black or from overseas have to endure.' He rejected Simmons's version of events as an 'utter falsehood'. The taunts, he added, were aimed at Cantona's nationality, sexual integrity and the sexual integrity of his mother. Provocation was 'serious and severe'. Mr Simmons had made a gesture denoting sexual self abuse. His client, meanwhile, was 'a man of positively good character acting out of character in a moment of extreme distress'. Cantona's charity work, letters of support for him, and the fact that his wife was pregnant were all raised. In view of his client's punishments so far – £10,800 (two weeks' wages), the FA suspension until 30 September and a further fine of £10,000 – Mr Poole called for a conditional discharge.

Mrs Pearch interrupted only occasionally for clarification. What was the weather like on the night in question, she wondered. Do modern footballers still wear studs? At least she seemed more informed than the judge who once asked in court who Paul Gascoigne was and whether this Gazza was famous. Then there was a more probing enquiry: 'Were these letters of support solicited?' she asked.

With her two fellow magistrates, Brian Chapman and Chris Funnell, Mrs Pearch then considered the evidence for an hour before returning with their verdict at 11.47 a.m. She began by announcing that there would be no costs and no compensation for Simmons, which raised hopes in the Cantona camp. They had, she said, taken into account Cantona's plea of guilty, his apologies and previous good character. Then, with the court rapt and faces tightening, she issued the following stunning words. 'We do feel, however, that you are a high-profile public figure with undoubted gifts, and you are looked up to by many young people. For this reason, the only sentence that is appropriate is two weeks' imprisonment forthwith.' He would be sent down to High Down, a category B prison a few miles away in Sutton.

There were gasps from the public gallery, which contained fans who had queued since dawn for a place. There was also one hiss of 'yes'. Cantona, wearing black trousers, grey T-shirt and a stylish blue jacket without lapels that, forlornly, bore a badge of the Statue of Liberty, looked shocked and silently sought the eyes of Paul Ince for reassurance, as he had Alex Ferguson's on that night. There could be none. When a French interpreter confirmed to Cantona the sentence, he half-smiled wryly and stepped backwards. Mr Poole, meanwhile, moved swiftly forwards. His application for immediate bail was refused and so he hurried to the adjacent Crown Court building to lodge an appeal and another application for bail.

Cantona was led to the cells, where he sat on a bench for some two and a half hours with his French lawyer Jean-Jacques Bertrand for company. Although it was his first time in prison, it must have seemed a familiar experience. He had, after all, spent long periods on the bench at Leeds United. He refused the offer of lunch – sausage and onions and spotted dick with custard – from the court canteen. Perhaps that, too, reminded him of Leeds. Finally, the appeal was granted in chambers by Judge Ian Davies and Cantona was released on a surety of £500. The appeal would be heard in eight days' time.

When he emerged into the sunshine at just after 3 p.m., reaction was mixed. Many cheered, some of them wearing Manchester United replica shirts. Cantona paused to sign autographs for two young girls, perhaps those who had been sobbing when they heard the verdict, before Ned Kelly escorted him back through an even more intense media scrum to the hotel. As local Crystal Palace sympathizers shouted 'Scum' and chanted 'Going down, going down, going down', Cantona clung to Kelly's arm. On his left, a woman PC acted as a bodyguard.

In his hotel room Cantona phoned his wife Isabelle, while downstairs Maurice Watkins deflected the media heat from him. 'Eric reacted to the sentence with calm and dignity but was clearly upset,' he said. Eric, he added, was looking forward to relaxing before the appeal after a 'harrowing' day.

As Cantona was driven back to Manchester, the reaction breaking all around him was a cocktail of mostly bitter ingredients, ranging from distasteful gloating and glee, to shock and outrage. 'Jailed then bailed. Kung-fu Cantona escapes a sending off', was Sky News's immediate headline. On the station, Paddy Crerand was going through his repertoire. 'It's disgraceful,' he bellowed. 'The media hype has a lot to do with it. They want people to be crucified. Three tinpot magistrates are trying to make a name for themselves. They couldn't have been any tougher on Eric Cantona than what they have been. This means that any hooligan can do what they like inside a stadium.' There was a good point in there somewhere, even if Cantona's sentence could have been worse: the maximum penalty for assault is six months' imprisonment and a £5000 fine.

Crerand did not broadcast the anecdote he had told Jean-Philippe Leclaire of *L'Équipe* magazine. 'I was sent off six times,' the talented former United midfield hard man said. 'One day I was going back to the dressing room to take the early shower when some bloke sought me out in the tunnel. I stuck my fist straight in his face. And because in those days no bloody television cameras were around to poke their noses in everywhere, nobody ever knew . . .'

Back in Croydon, even the prosecutor in the case, Jeffrey McCann, had been surprised at the attention it had all attracted. When he had emerged from the court in the morning he apparently told waiting reporters: 'I did the gay serial killer case, and there was nowhere near the interest in that. I've never seen so many media people. There are cameras on cranes here.'

Across London, it should have been one of the proudest days of Alex Ferguson's life. Resplendent in his specially commissioned kilt, he was at Buckingham Palace to receive his Commander of the British Empire award for services to football in the New Year's Honours List. Her Majesty was making his day while her representatives were marring it. He was too stunned to comment; besides which, he was preoccupied with somewhat sadder news, the death due to a brain haemorrhage of Davie Cooper, the outstanding Rangers and Scotland winger, at the age of thirty-nine.

Others were not so reticent. That night, even *Newsnight* dipped its toes into the sporting waters and the Leeds United fan Jeremy Paxman — famed for an interview technique that recalls Billy Bremner's playing style — chaired a discussion among lawyers. Michael Mansfield QC felt Cantona's was a harsh punishment. Three paratroopers in Aldershot were recently convicted of an unprovoked assault on a civilian, he pointed out, and had received community service. Keith Richard, the guitarist with the Rolling Stones, had been forced to organize a concert for the needy when he was found guilty of an offence. 'All the court's done has been to become a pawn in the media game,' he added. This stems from a much greater malaise. The real thing is what is going on in society, this insidious infiltration into the terraces. 'It was not wise, he said to hold up a sentence *"pour encourager les autres".'*

Indeed, the mood changed, with considerable sympathy being extended to Cantona. 'I thought everyone was equal in the eyes of the law,' Gordon Taylor, the chief executive of the Professional

Footballers' Association, pointed out simply and pertinently. 'Cantona could have expected a sentence that would not have put him in custody,' said Steven Kay of the Criminal Bar Association. 'He has been made an example of.'

Therein was to lie the error of judgement by Mrs Pearch, a 53-year-old retired music teacher, chairman of Croydon magistrates for less than three months after serving as a deputy for two years, and who had been selected to hear the case because she had no interest in football.

'The following day the mood discerned by a reviewer of the French press on Radio 5 was 'What can you expect from an English court judging a Frenchman?'

The British press was at its varied best and worst. The *Daily Telegraph*'s cartoonist Matt, with his ability to wring comforting humour from the most hysterical of stories, drew a judge with gavel poised, shouting: 'Two, four, six, eight, who do we incarcerate . . .' The *Sun*, meanwhile, won the award for wittiest headline of the morning with 'Ooh-aah, Prisona' but little merit for its hawkish coverage thereafter. 'Fair tackle, Mrs Pearch,' said its leader, for this was a story too big for just the sports and news pages. 'A thug is still a thug whether he earns £100 or £10,000 a week,' it said. 'Everyone who loves soccer owes a debt of gratitude to magistrate Mrs Jean Pearch . . . Soccer must grow up. It has a responsibility towards the millions of youngsters who copy everything their heroes do. Watch a school match and you'll be horrified at the fouls, dissent and bad sportsmanship. That's the shameful legacy of men like Cantona.'

On another page, though, they did carry the reaction of Mrs Kathy Churchman, the woman who had been closest to the incident: 'When I heard he was going to prison I just screamed out: "I can't believe it." I thought he might get a suspended sentence. He deserved to be punished, but not prison.'

It was left to the somewhat more doveish *Guardian* to put matters in perspective. Their leader, headlined 'Ooh-aah: a jail sentence too far', pointed out that common assault is a serious offence but not one that requires notification to the Home Office for inclusion in the violent crime statistics. According to figures: of

8500 guilty verdicts in 1993, 2800 were fined, 3700 were discharged, 1450 given a probation order, 430 a community service order and 337 – under four per cent – sent to prison.

'Mrs Pearch has breached a fundamental principle of the 1991 Criminal Justice Act,' the paper said, 'and ridden roughshod over the Magistrates' Association's guidance. Parliament has made it clear that prison must be reserved for offences so serious that only prison is justified. Cantona's kick does not fall into that category.' Cantona, it added, passed every one of the seven separate grounds which magistrates are supposed to consider in calculating the seriousness of an offence. 'It was not premeditated; in a group action; committed on bail; by a person in authority; against a vulnerable victim or a public servant; and there were no previous convictions.'

For the football writers, the question to be considered was whether this would tip Cantona over the edge and force him to leave the country with which he had supposedly been enjoying a love affair. He had not, after all, been known to stay where he did not feel wanted; wanted above all others. When the going had got tough, he had got going and Internazionale were still prepared to make the going good.

His Manchester United team-mates feared the worst. There was 'total devastation' within the ranks, said the captain Steve Bruce. 'It seems to us that he is being made a scapegoat for so many other things,' he added, referring to the manifold other ills of the game at the time. 'I can't believe he is being given a jail sentence for what he did. I feel so sorry for Eric and so sorry for his family.' Said Lee Sharpe: 'I just don't know if he will be prepared to put up with any more after this latest decision.' It remained true, though, that he was having to put up with what he himself had set in motion.

The United chief executive Martin Edwards was angry. 'This is a shock. The whole thing has got out of hand,' he said. 'If we had known what the courts and FA were going to do to him at the beginning, we would not have been so tough.' That was a parochial view. 'We took very stringent action when we banned him until the end of the season. We also imposed the maximum fine, but then the FA deemed it necessary to extend the ban. Now this is a third punishment – for one offence.'

Those closest to Cantona were divided as to what his reaction might be, which probably reflected Cantona's own pendulous state of mind. No matter how foolish he had been, how reckless and ridiculous, it was hard not to feel sympathy for a man in a foreign country at the mercy of the courts. Jean-Jacques Bertrand said Cantona had given him no indication that he wanted to leave. 'He is a Manchester United player and I am sure he will remain so,' he said. 'He has not said to me at any stage up to now that he wants to leave. These things can happen. You can be in any country, whether it is England, France or Japan, and something will trouble you. It could be something like this. It could be driving your car too fast. Eric does not see it as a reason to leave England and neither do I.'

By contrast, in Paris Jean-Jacques Amorfini of the French players' union, and Cantona's agent, was certain that Cantona would quit. 'They are all out to get him and I can tell you that he won't stay in that country a lot longer,' he said on French radio. 'I think people are trying to make Cantona disgusted with England and, obviously, I believe he is going to have to leave the country.' He also felt that Cantona had been badly advised. 'We are dumbfounded and absolutely shocked because Manchester United's English lawyers advised a guilty plea so English justice would show clemency.'

Where could Cantona go? Not back to France, surely. Spain? Johan Cruyff had said that he was an admirer of the boy who had admired him but that he would not be right for his Barcelona team. Italy offered one outlet. Inter were still on Cantona's trail, their dogged new owner Massimo Moratti waiting for any development. In the meantime, the appeal at Croydon would be crucial.

He had, at least, to stay for that. And when he returned to Croydon eight days later, to the Crown rather than magistrates court, the circus was back in town. This time, the high-wire artist was dressed rather less trendily, more soberly, probably on lawyers' advice, probably on the basis that judges have been known to look more kindly on those appearing externally respectable. Now Cantona was wearing dark trousers, a grey cashmere jacket, black waistcoat, white shirt and spotted tie. The light brown boots retained the hint of rebellion, but then they were not visible from the dock. He had apparently enjoyed another night out before the hearing but this time was back at his hotel at 1.30 a.m.

First the prosecution went over the old ground of the facts of, as police and judicial statements always say, 'the night in question'. They of course had nothing new to add, but Mr Mark Dennis – whose name may have raised a wry smile, his namesake in football having been something of an ill-disciplined full-back in a spell with, among others, Crystal Palace – outlined anew the distress caused to women and children.

At this point Cantona was passed a card in the dock by one of the twenty Manchester United supporters allowed access to the public gallery. It came from thirteen-year-old Sebastian Pennells, wearing a blue and white United third strip, who with his mother Zoe had left home in Sevenoaks, Kent, at 5.30 a.m. to get a place. Master Pennells later revealed to reporters the poem it contained:

> Eric is an idol,
> Eric is a star,
> And if my mother had her way,
> He'd also be my Pa.

It wasn't quite the Baudelaire or Rimbaud that Cantona was used to. It remained unopened for the moment: if and when he did note the contents, he would also have read a request for him not to leave Manchester United.

This time the defence had rather more to offer. Armed with the Home Office figures quoted in the *Guardian* leader, David Poole QC pointed out that jail sentences for such an offence were rare and that the magistrate had 'acted apparently contrary to statute'. Clearly, he added, the lay bench was telling Cantona he was going to prison 'not because the offence was so serious that only a custodial sentence was appropriate, but because of his high profile and the way in which he was regarded. It was a judgement that was not only flawed but contrary to the clearly expressed will of Parliament. It therefore was not open to the bench to rely on the appellant's high profile as justification for sending him to prison.'

Mr Poole also added a new twist. 'As the bench said last week, he is looked up to by the young. In that case he has offered them the finest of examples. He has told the truth. He has co-operated with the police. He has admitted he was entirely in the wrong. He has apologized. He has pleaded guilty. These are wonderful lessons for the young and he has given them all.' It became clearer; Cantona's act was in fact designed to be a lesson to the young. He hadn't, after all, done all those things simply because he needed to if he was to stay out of jail.

'These proceedings have come as a great shock to him and his family,' Mr Poole continued. 'He has resolved that whatever provocation may present itself in future he will never again act this way or in any comparable way.' Cantona was, he added, 'just as likely to be hurt when abused, just as likely to fail in a crisis, as he did here, and just as likely to feel ashamed when he lets himself down'. So the messiah was just as human as the rest of us.

Judge Ian Davies retired for thirty minutes and when he returned, his remarks before announcing his verdict were clearly more sympathetic than had been the magistrate's. Cantona, he said, had been confronted with behaviour which would 'provoke the most stoic, and we believe that Mr Cantona reacted in a way that was out of character. We believe he would not have done so but for the provocative conduct aimed at him.' He added that he hoped Cantona would 'be used in carrying out his public duty to the community by helping young people who aspire to be professional footballers and others who merely aspire to play the game and enjoy it'.

The verdict was 120 hours of community service; he would meet probation officers in Manchester the following Monday to work out how to approach it. Cantona was asked if he understood and with a faint smile playing on his lips he shrugged his shoulders

and replied, 'Oui.' A repressed 'yes' went up in the public gallery
– a United one this week – and there was applause. Two women
in United kit wept. One of them, 39-year-old Gillian Priest, who
had also been in tears at the first hearing, moved to hug Cantona
in the dock and kiss the hand of his barrister. Cantona shook hands
with several supporters and raised an arm in acknowledgement to
others.

Leaving court a free man, the inevitable clique of cameras
besieged Cantona on the walk back to the Croydon Park Hotel,
Ned Kelly and police in attendance. United supporters cheered
but a group of Palace fans shouting 'French scum' and 'Fuck off
back to France' were kept at a distance by police.

Cantona, in private consultation with Maurice Watkins, agreed
to appear at a press conference at the hotel. He knew what he
wanted to say: '*Quand les mouettes suivent le chalutier, c'est parce
qu'elles espèrent qu'on leur jette des poissons.*' He discussed it with
Watkins. 'What,' he asked Watkins, 'do you call in English those
sea birds?' 'Do you mean seagulls?' Watkins wondered. 'Yes. And
those boats that go fishing?' 'Trawlers, perhaps,' ventured Watkins. 'And the fish that they use?' Watkins was trying to think of
sprats but came up instead with sardines. And so was fashioned
one of the most bizarre and celebrated of sporting quotations.

Do you have anything to say, asked the press?

'When the seagulls follow the trawler,' Cantona began somewhat nervously before pausing to take a sip of water, 'it is because
they think sardines will be thrown into the sea,' he announced.
The 'thank you very much' was all but lost as he rose to leave.
The press conference dissolved into laughter and the newspapers
had a field day.

'Fish-quoter Cantona ducks the cells,' read a *Guardian* headline.
'Cantona free, philosophy nil,' said the *Daily Telegraph*, in which
Ben Fenton wrote: 'With a display of impenetrability that most
soccer defences would die for, Eric Cantona eschewed discussion
of his escape from the threat of jail yesterday in favour of a one-
sided critique of commercial fishing.' In the *Independent* Simon
Midgley reported that 'Eric Cantona, footballing genius, poet and
cod philosopher-king was as gnomic as a sphinx.' The *Sun* was

Above More grief, against
England in Sweden, 1992.
(Christian Liewig/Popperfoto)

Right Merde! Cantona blamed
Ginola ... Ginola denied all
responsibility ... The team
turned on the Parisian crowd ...
The crowd blamed the team.
Just some of the fallout from
Bulgaria's last-minute goal
which prevented France from
flying to the USA. *(Colorsport)*

Overleaf In control and
advancing upon
worried-looking
colleagues at The Cliff
training ground. The
L'Équipe photo that hints
at a fruitful future
partnership with Cole.
(Presse-Sports/Empics)

Above The red and the
Blackburn: the last goal
before Selhurst Park.
(Colorsport)

Left Wot, no more games
this season? E.C. was
here, celebrating the
Blackburn goal.
(Colorsport)

Right Abused, amused and
avenged: Mr Simmons
delivers, Mrs Churchman
smiles, Monsieur Cantona
responds.
(Popperfoto; Steve Lindsell)

Left The morning after the night before. *(Popperfoto)*

Right Courting the cameras: Cantona live at Croydon. *(Popperfoto)*

Below 'Quand les mouettes suivent le chalutier, c'est parce qu'elles espèrent qu'on leur jette des poissons.' *(Colorsport)*

Master of all he surveys … *(Steve Lindsell)*

unwilling to enter into any esoteric discussion. 'Ooh-aah, it's mad you are,' they said.

What could it all mean? Was the reference to Seagulls a sign that Cantona intended to quit United and sign for Brighton and Hove Albion? Was it a topical political statement about the dispute going on between Spanish fishermen and Canada? Or was Cantona pining for the *bouillabaisse* dish so popular in the Marseille region?

Simply, it referred to the media pack expecting tasty titbits from the mouth of a man they hoped would be condemned. He was neither condemned nor willing to provide them with any more morsels. 'It was an obscure thing to say,' admitted Maurice Watkins. 'He just does not want to stay here and meet you and answer questions, because he has had enough. I think he has been under tremendous strain. I think that gives you some example of the extreme pressure that Eric Cantona has been under with this case.' The *Sun*, with a little licence perhaps, additionally reported Watkins as saying: 'All he wants is to eat lunch – hopefully a little bigger than a sardine.'

The *Daily Mail* did their own trawling. They reported a psychologist called Raj Persaud as saying: 'He wants to keep people guessing because he thinks he is better than everyone else . . . Behind the remark are his feelings of being superior . . . He doesn't like being ignored.' Professor Percy Cohen, apparently a 'psychology and rationality lecturer' at the London School of Economics, said that the remarks illustrated 'pure defiance. The man is saying "I will be back and I will be back a stronger man, and in charge of what I am doing." It is really quite eloquent and shows that he is not mad at all, despite what everyone might think.' Dr Dinah Burch, a fellow in English at Trinity College, Oxford, added: 'It is impossible to say whether he has any literary talent on this one verse but it is a clever response nevertheless.' 'This is something I have heard before,' said Fabien Ousselot, London correspondent of *Libération*, dismissively at the press conference.

On the wider, more important question of justice being done, it seemed that Cantona had, in football's parlance, got the right result. A man who had been close to the original incident, James Mulligan, with his five-year-old son, said: 'My son knows what Cantona did was wrong but through a child's eyes prison is only for really bad people, and Cantona is not bad. He just over-reacted. Jail was a daft sentence. Thank goodness common sense prevailed. Now children can benefit from his community service work.' Added Kathy Churchman: 'Prison was too harsh. This is ideal.'

Perhaps so, but perhaps also the court could have gone further and shown more enlightenment. There was the option, as occurs in the United States, of insisting on some form of counselling in anger management. In the case of Paul Merson, who had admitted his addiction to alcohol and gambling, the FA had decided that rehabilitative treatment rather than mere punishment was preferable. In Cantona's case there was the complication of some public demand for blood, and any argument against rehabilitative treatment would chime with the conventional wisdom that to try to tame him would be to douse the fire in his belly, and he would not be the player he was. Cantona himself was unconventional, however. It may have been that some form of counselling could empower rather than emasculate him; allow him to express his talent without the rage that had hitherto so undermined his career.

Still the debate as to whether Cantona would leave England raged on. The verdict may have gone his way but the experience had been so distasteful and demoralizing that it was on a knife edge. Matters were hardly helped the weekend following the appeal when Cantona, Isabelle and Raphaël were told that they had three days to vacate the house in Worsley rented for them by Manchester United. The owner, a Mr Michael Higgins, was returning from Spain and United's efforts to buy the £80,000 house – they themselves valuing it at a lot less – had fallen through. As had efforts to extend the lease so that the heavily pregnant Isabelle would not have to endure the upheaval of a move. It was back to a hotel near Manchester airport. Still, Cantona at least was used to it. For his first year with United, he had occupied room 216 at the Novotel West on the days when he could not face the drive back to the family home they'd retained in Leeds, where Isabelle taught.

The next weekend, United were playing Crystal Palace in the semi-final of the FA Cup. On the Saturday, the day before the match, Richard Shaw, the defender at the centre of the sending off that had led to the incident, spoke out. He told how he had received hate mail from Cantona devotees holding him responsible for getting their hero dismissed, accusing him of doing so deliberately. There had been threats against him and his family, he added. 'I can only ask both sets of fans to go to the game with an open mind and don't end up spoiling it,' he urged.

It was a forlorn hope. Ninety minutes before the 4 p.m. kick-off came the scenes at the New Fullbrook pub in Walsall that led to the death of Palace fan Paul Nixon, crushed under the wheels of a coach. More than fifty fans were involved at one point, with knives brandished as well as fists and boots. A Palace supporters' coach was stoned. One man was stabbed. According to the chairman of the Crystal Palace Supporters' Club, Chris Plummer: 'The editor of one of the Crystal Palace fanzines was held up against a wall and was forced to sing Cantona songs.'

The match was drawn 2–2, United twice coming back from behind, but the death overshadowed the occasion. It meant a replay three days later; three days of hysteria later. On the day of the match both Alex Ferguson and Alan Smith appealed for calm. Twenty minutes before kick-off, the two managers appeared on the pitch to plead for order, to remember that this was only a game. 'A club like Manchester United, with its history and traditions, demands the best behaviour on and off the pitch,' said Ferguson in an interview with David Davies, a BBC television reporter before joining the FA, on a microphone from the centre circle.

Few were there to hear it; the crowd of 17,987 was the lowest ever for an FA Cup semi-final. It was an eerie sight. Most Palace fans, disgusted, had boycotted the match. United's remained defiant. 'Ooh-aah, Cantona,' went the familiar refrain, perhaps as a message to their talisman not to leave the club, but still crassly insensitive. It had been the chant that had started the trouble in

Walsall and indirectly caused the fatality. The Palace director Colin
Noades, brother of chief executive Ron, went to the stadium manager to protest, to seek a tannoy announcement denouncing it. It
was felt, instead, that it might incite more. Besides which, no
matter how distasteful, free speech can never be suppressed nor
football grounds sanitized. Not fully anyway.

On the pitch, a routine 2–0 win for United was marred by a
moment of madness. Roy Keane, upset by a hard but fair tackle
from Darren Pitcher had required seven stitches in his ankle at
half-time. In the second half he was still bristling and tangled with
Gareth Southgate, then responded to a lunging tackle from the
Palace captain by stamping twice on his stomach. The immediate
image that sprang to mind was that of Cantona and John Moncur
at Swindon at a similarly frantic stage of the previous season. A
new bout of Cantona chanting followed; the United fans revelling
in their 'no one likes us, we don't care' attitude of late. A mêlée
of players developed, after which Keane was sent off, along with
Palace's Darren Patterson who had waded into Keane.

In the interview room afterwards, Alex Ferguson looked almost
at his wit's end. Mark Saggers of Sky Television News asked him
whether on this of all nights, having urged restraint for the game,
he was now willing to condemn Keane's actions. Ferguson conceded that Keane's action had been silly and that he deserved his
sending off. Pressed for something more contrite, Ferguson grew
angry. United's disciplinary system was conducted privately, not
publicly, he insisted. 'None of you have been football managers,'
he snapped. 'You don't know what it's like.' Ferguson had once
complained to a sports editor about a journalist who published
some off-the-record comments, but the editor had stood by his
man. It was the same with him and his United team, his family.
'What happened in private, I don't know,' Ferguson added. Nor
did we when it came to United.

In the car park, separated by iron railings from fans willing to
wait long after the final whistle for autographs, the United players
conducted interviews in the darkness and looked bemused anew
by this latest blow to the club's esteem. In a corner, Erik
Bielderman of *L'Équipe* took Alex Ferguson aside from the ever-

present TV cameras to ask whether Cantona was going or staying. He did not yet know himself; only Eric knew, he replied. He and his team should have been enjoying the moment of reaching an FA Cup Final. Instead they were defending themselves. Eric Cantona was miles away, no doubt in touch with the night's events, but his presence still loomed large throughout the whole evening.

It was a point taken up by the columnists in the morning. 'Scarred by the ghost of Cantona,' said the *Sun*'s headline. 'Ferguson has been criticized for his refusal to sack Cantona,' wrote John Sadler. 'Now he has been forced to watch one of his own stars putting the boot into an opponent on a night that carried memories of the Frenchman's dreadful contribution to United's proud history.'

In the *Daily Telegraph* Donald Trelford wondered again whether Cantona would stay or should stay. Under the headline 'Reckless Eric must soon be on his way' he wrote: 'Manchester United fans are already blaming Eric Cantona for their likely failure to retain the Premiership title. His absence disrupted their rhythm at a crucial phase of the season and for that reason, if for no other, I do not think he will play again at Old Trafford.' He concluded: 'I think Cantona is a nasty piece of work and English football will be well rid of him.' A move from the owlish *Observer* to the bullish *Telegraph* had clearly affected Trelford.

Doubts were also being raised about whether there would be a law-enforcement problem in such a climate should Cantona appear again. This was the relevant question. Tony Kershaw, chairman of the National Federation of Supporters' Clubs, believed there would be 'near-anarchy' were he to appear again at an English ground.

'He will be baited by fans and goaded by rival players,' said Kershaw. 'Referees will have a nightmare, especially if he is closely involved in a challenge for the ball; for some players cheat. The reaction he will get is unacceptable as far as I'm concerned. It is too big a price for the game to pay and I don't think he should play in this country again. I enjoy watching Cantona play and I understand why United want him to stay. But the club couldn't handle George Best and I don't think they can handle Eric

Cantona. The only way the situation could be resolved is if Cantona controlled his temper. That's a miraculous dream as far as I am concerned. It's not as if he's been sent off just once. He's constantly been involved in trouble as he has a very short fuse.'

That March, Cantona occupied himself as best he could: kicking off a benefit match back in France for a supporter stabbed at a club match; watching the World Ice Skating Championships at the NEC in Birmingham, in particular the elegant Surya Bonaly. Now, between return forays to France, he would be spending his time in a gloomy hotel overlooking the M56, just a few hundred yards from a check-in desk at Ringway airport, venturing out to train with his team-mates and do his time in community service. His mind was clearly weighing up the alternative of Milan. He must have been sorely tempted to stroll up to the departure terminal and check out for good.

8   Re-united

They keep me from all trespass grave,
They guide my steps towards the Beautiful;
They are my servants and I am their slave;
This living flame I follow heart and soul.
Charles Baudelaire, 'The Living Flame'
(from *Spleen and Ideal*)

The Manchester United chief executive Martin Edwards received
a phone call from Milan early in the New Year of 1995 requesting
a meeting. It came from Paolo Taveggia, an aide to Internazionale's new owner, Massimo Moratti. He had been instructed
– yes, 'instructed' – by Signor Moratti to sign Eric Cantona and
Paul Ince. Edwards told him that there was little chance of United
selling either but, out of curiosity and courtesy, he agreed to a
meeting. He was a businessman, after all. A date was set for a
London hotel: 26 January, 1995. It would be convenient as United
were in town the night before.

   Inter had for several years been living with, but in the shadow
of, AC Milan, with whom they shared the imposing Giuseppe
Meazza Stadium, which resembles the mother ship in *Close
Encounters of the Third Kind*, in the San Siro district of the city.
Silvio Berlusconi, media magnate and latterly Prime Minister of
Italy after setting up his own Forza Italia party – the name taken

from the traditional football chant of Italian *tifosi* – had poured in millions to make Milan the most successful, most admired and most revered club in the world game. To their outstanding home defensive talents such as Franco Baresi and Paolo Maldini they had added the flamboyant attacking brio of the Dutch trio Ruud Gullit, Frank Rijkaard and Marco Van Basten. In the nineties AC Milan made the Championship their own and, under Berlusconi's patronage, had won three European Cups to go with two previously. Inter had retaliated by signing the German threesome Jürgen Klinsmann, Lothar Matthäus and Andreas Brehme, and for a while a thrilling rivalry was established. Inter, though, were always second best. It had been thirty years since they had won a European Cup. A UEFA Cup in 1993–94 simply was not good enough.

Moratti, who had made his money in the petrochemical industry, was determined to make an impact and ready to put his money where his mouth was. Ince was the new Frank Rijkaard he declared; Cantona was to be the striker who pulled it together. Moratti was unconcerned by his reputation. 'My concerns are with the skill and brain of a player,' he said. 'Cantona is a cultured man and super class.' The Dutch duo of Wim Jonk and Dennis Bergkamp currently on the books were deemed replaceable by the Manchester United axis.

Moratti, Taveggia, who was to become Inter's chief executive, and Gianmaria Visconti Modrone, another aide, watched the Palace game from what passed as VIP seats at Selhurst Park, not far from the incident. They were not put off by Cantona's moment of madness nor Ince's alleged part in its aftermath and Taveggia and Visconti Modrone turned up the following morning (Moratti remained at his hotel) at the Royal Lancaster Hotel, close to FA headquarters.

Edwards politely listened to what Taveggia had to say and was moderately interested by the sum of money being mentioned, possibly £10 million for the pair. There could be no transfers without Alex Ferguson's agreement, however, Edwards announced. Besides which, the Inter party may have noticed that

United had had a little trouble at Selhurst Park the night before, which may have changed the picture a little.

If anything, the events at Crystal Palace, along with the disciplinary hearing and the court cases, enhanced Inter's chances of getting their men. The pendulum had been swinging wildly from 'yes he will stay' to 'oh no he won't' for two months when Martin Edwards finally sat down on Monday 10 April with Jean-Jacques Bertrand – Cantona was spending a long weekend in France – for talks about a new contract to replace the one that had a year to run. It was the day after the Palace fan had died in Walsall.

It was to be ironic how matters eventually unfolded. At first, United had informed Inter that Ince was simply not available. He was an English player, the hub of their team, and they needed all the English players they could get for European competition. The stance on Cantona may have modified a little, however. Here was a player, nearly 29, with a year left on his contract and over whom there was uncertainty as to whether he would again be able to exist, let alone thrive, in the hothouse atmosphere his return to the Premiership was certain to engender. United maintained publicly, though, that they were keen to keep him.

Edwards's talks with Bertrand lasted ninety minutes, and it was a somewhat downbeat chief executive who emerged. Cantona had always insisted that money was not the main motivation for him, but it was clear that he knew his worth. Inter were apparently ready to pay United a transfer fee of some £5.5 million and Cantona wages of £25,000 a week. United simply could not match that but were willing to break their pay structure to double, at least, his current basic wage of £5400 a week. It is believed that Bertrand raised the subject of his client sharing in some of the profits on the large amounts of merchandise sold bearing Cantona's name, but United refused point-blank.

The biggest issue was whether Cantona felt able to continue in England. 'I'm optimistic, but I think a lot depends on where Eric wants to be,' said Edwards. 'If Eric wants to play for United he is certainly going to get a very good offer from us.' One, in fact, that with bonuses and signing fees could amount to as much as £15,000 a week. 'If he feels that he has had enough of England, or perhaps that he is in an impossible position, then that's a different matter. But we'll be doing our best to retain him.' A feeling that Cantona might be ready to quit was confirmed by Bertrand. 'The circumstances are very hard for Cantona to handle. It is now all very difficult for Eric,' he said.

Indeed, two days later, on the morning of the semi-final replay against Crystal Palace, the *Daily Mirror*'s chief kite-flyer Harry Harris reported that Cantona had already decided to accept Inter's offer. The fee would be £4.5 million, Cantona's three-year contract worth £3 million. It was, however, wrong. No substantiating quote from anyone involved was offered in the piece, no sources named. If he had got it right, he could have triumphantly reproduced the page containing the story with 'We told you first' headlines – called a rag-out, in the trade – but in the event everyone forgot. It is only chip paper, after all.

Cantona, meanwhile, had begun his community service. In the mornings, he would train with United as usual at The Cliff before hosting two-hour sessions for local children in the afternoon, overseen by a probation officer, who insisted that this was no soft option for Cantona. The first to benefit were Ellesmere Park Juniors, a team of 9–11-year-olds based in Eccles. They were one of fourteen clubs involved with the Salford Community Link Project. In all, Cantona would teach more than 600 boys and girls. 'I cannot express how thrilled we are to have been selected for coaching by a football genius,' said Les Harris, the club's manager.

When Saturday Comes then ran an amusing front cover with the line 'Cantona goes to work'. Under it was a picture of Cantona's team-mates Steve Bruce and Gary Pallister smiling. 'Sir, sir, can I be in your class?' said the bubble coming from Bruce's mouth. 'My sister fancies you!' was attributed to Pallister.

Anything on Cantona was now big, and news editors took anything on him, no matter how ridiculous. On a return trip to France he apparently appeared on a television show about people with famous relatives. Brother Jean-Marie told a series of fibs, one being that Eric was taught football to wean him off dolls. He was baffled but still remained cool when a member of the audience began heckling. He then burst into laughter when he realized it was all a prank. Then there was the tale of a 29-year-old man in Cornwall who used a poster of Cantona to scare an owl from his window ledge and, in a publicity stunt, Gary Lineker was said to have been lined up to kung-fu kick an old lady for his 'No more Mr Nice Guy' potato crisps ad campaign.

A computer-game company also announced plans for a package titled *Parlez-vous Kung-fu?*, which featured a skinhead footballer called Ernie Container kicking out at a hooligan. And a group of United fans got together to produce a record of 'Ooh-aah, Cantona' (Go West version) and 'Eric the King' (to the tune of 'Lily the Pink'). It was, said the blurb, 'issued in a spirit of positive defiance against the unjust treatment of Eric Cantona . . . It's an ethnomusicological field recording featuring the rich oral history indigenous to the terraces of Old Trafford.' Cantona would surely have understood that.

But it was more the reaction of the Les Harrises of the world, and the kids he taught, which touched Cantona and would have a powerful effect on his decision whether or not to stay in England. He realized again how strong was his attachment to the country, that it was not the frustrating unforgiving place he perceived it to be during the dark days of early spring. He realized, too, how strong was the attachment of his fans to him, and the affinity of children for him.

When Cantona personally met with Edwards on Monday 24 April, the talks on this occasion lasted an astonishing eleven hours. And this time Edwards emerged more optimistic. Matters were still unresolved, however. Both sides were anxious that the issue did not spill into the summer and Cantona agreed that he would give United an answer by the end of the week. A press conference would be arranged for Friday morning to announce his decision.

It was *comme çi, comme ça* right to the last minute. The *Daily Mirror* reported again that Cantona had decided to go. He believed, they said, the abuse he would receive on away grounds would be too much for him to bear. The balance shifted the next day, when it emerged that Cantona had apparently indicated to Edwards that he would be staying. He had met with him on the Thursday night to iron out details.

'Hopefully everything will be tied up,' said Alex Ferguson. 'We hope we get a good response from Eric and will be able to announce a positive decision. I'm optimistic, and if we get the right decision tomorrow it will be terrific for us, the best news we have had at United for a long time. Eric has looked at all the angles, so have we, and the signs right now are good. It has been a trying time for everyone involved. There has been a lot of decision-making to be faced by Eric. We've also had to look at how we, as a club, can sort out various things next season. It's not going to be easy but we'll have to review our own security at away games.'

Even Ferguson was not certain, however, until 9.35 a.m. the following morning, Friday 28 April, when Cantona walked into his office and announced to the manager that, yes, he had indeed decided to stay. Cantona's fashion statement that day was blue jeans, a red T-shirt and a red-and-white candy-striped jacket. And a Take That baseball cap.

It thus became clear thirty-five minutes later that, with Cantona striding purposefully into the suite set aside at Old Trafford for the press conference, flanked by Martin Edwards and Alex Ferguson and having eschewed the cap, he had retaken his marriage vows. As Sky News cameras rolled to bring live coverage, Edwards announced that the new three-year contract would run until June 1988 (a slip of the tongue; the market leaders of the nineties were certainly not a club living in the past). He was delighted at the outcome and pointed out that Cantona had now been punished four-fold: by United; by the FA; by the courts and by the French Football Federation. (This was clearly to pre-empt anyone pointing out that here was a man who was profiting from notoriety rather than being sacked, as many had called for.) It had been, Edwards continued, a long, traumatic period. 'We hope this brings it all to an end.' We would see. The following Sunday, assessing his £750,000-a-year contract, the *Observer*'s sports cartoonist Bradford drew Cantona saying: 'I think, therefore I am rich.' It later emerged that the deal had a pay-as-you-play element, with Cantona only receiving his full salary if he was actually available.

After Edwards came a word or two from the trawler captain, this time willing to scatter a few sardines. Why, in the face of so much hostility, had he decided to stay? 'Why? Because Manchester United are the biggest club in England, maybe in Europe, maybe the world.' Was he pleased at the outcome? A rare smile broke out. 'I'm very pleased to have the opportunity in the next three years to win many trophies with them. Everybody at this club deserves this, and the fans too. I have never thought about leaving United, never. There are some people in England I thought about leaving, but nobody at this club. There was a difficult moment for me once when I thought about joining Inter Milan. It was a short moment, though. I am happy to spend the rest of my career at Old Trafford. We are bigger than the people who have been so hard and so wrong sometimes. I can forget everything now, even the criticism, because I know we can win everything.'

He began to relax in a rather less intimidating atmosphere than he had been used to over the last few months. 'This has been a love story. It is something that is very strong for me. The love of the club is the most important weapon in the world. I just couldn't leave,' he added. There was a hint, too, of the opposite side of the coin. 'People fear me more than I fear them,' he said enigmatically.

The inquisitors turned to Ferguson, again uncomfortable in the glare of live television cameras and news reporters. 'We were never going to win in this situation, whatever we did,' he said. 'But this is a giant step towards winning things. We have never had a complaint from Eric about his punishments: he never said a word. He has handled it all so well.' He believed, he added, that the onus was now on fans to behave themselves.

More was required from Cantona on this rare opportunity to speak to him in person. Would he spend the rest of his career at Old Trafford? 'Yes, I hope so.' Did he feel he would be able to cope with the hostility that would inevitably return when he did? 'Yes. Easy.' Hmm. Then he sought permission to leave, pointing to his watch. 'Please excuse me, I have to be at training,' he said. For a match in October, someone pointed out. The conference ended with a smile. More usually they had ended, metaphorically at least, in tears.

Someone then forgot to phone Internazionale. Paolo Taveggia, on hearing the news, claimed that United had told them Cantona would be their player. 'I am disappointed with Cantona's representatives, his manager and his lawyer,' he said. 'They were not as fair with us as we were with them. We were waiting for a phone call from his representatives but they did not bother to call us.'

Ferguson, though, did talk further to the football correspondents and took them aside, clearly wanting to expand on the subject of the responsibility of supporters. He also wanted a wider public to know that it had been made clear to Cantona during contract negotiations that anything resembling a repeat of the Selhurst Park incident would mean the end for him.

'I think Eric himself recognizes that this is the last chance for him in this country in terms of discipline,' he told the coterie. 'That's the case. No question about it. All those issues have to go through his mind now. Eric has to handle it now. He knows if he is sent off again everything will erupt once more. You know, he has just taken the hardest decision he could possibly have taken. The easiest option would have been to run away from all this. Instead, he has put himself in the firing line because this man Cantona has been prepared to say: "I am not going to let them beat me."

'We are going to get crucified for signing this player. There is nothing you can do about it, no way we can please everybody. All we can do in this situation is please ourselves, because we have taken more than enough stick in the last few months. For Eric it has taken tremendous courage to stay. A lot would have cracked under the intense scrutiny he has endured. Truthfully, I thought it was almost certain that Eric would go because it was going to be so difficult for him to remain here. Really you had to ask yourself whether it was right by him to even want him to stay. But I've watched closely how Eric has handled everything since it happened back in January. I have wondered, too, whether anyone in the world could have dealt with it. You never know how much the punishment has hurt him because he just seems to ride through it, handle it without a problem. But deep down you just don't know how it has got to him.'

Then it was on to the subject that most concerned him. 'All we can hope is everything is going to be right in the future. We hope there will be honesty towards him from other players in the game. Everyone wants to win, but how far they are prepared to go to win can vary. It's not going to be easy. Within every game there is going to be provocation, fans chanting every time he touches the ball.' He saw it as peculiar to English football that its characters were pilloried. 'When someone is doing well we have to knock him down. We don't do it with horses. Red Rum is more loved than anyone I know. Why is that? I've never heard a bad word said about Red Rum. But he must have lost one race.' Then again, they shoot horses, don't they?

A mood of hatred towards United had developed, more sinister than any previous rivalry, Ferguson believed. 'When you're at the top, people want to knock you down,' he said, voicing the inevitable (and fair-enough) consequence of being the most successful club in the country. But it was worse than that. 'Roy Evans said that even at Liverpool's height they were not hated nearly as much as Manchester United are now. We just don't know what we can do.' He had first noticed the hostility at West Ham a year earlier when home fans had shouted Judas at their former player Paul Ince and thrown bananas at him. They remained upset, five years on, that Ince had been photographed in a United shirt long before any transfer; that he had engineered a move. 'It was unbelievable,' said Ferguson. 'Even in the FA Cup Final Chelsea fans were throwing things at Ryan Giggs when he was taking corners.

'Before and after the games is terrible. The disappointing thing for spectators is that because of the way it has become, players can't stop to give autographs to these wee kids standing at the front of the bus. You can't stop nowadays. You've got to get in the coach and get your head down. Come October,' he added, 'I would think that we wouldn't come off the coach until we get a clear passage.' He wanted to see, he said, players' entrances cordoned off with steel frames. It was a sad reflection of the way the game was going.

United would take their own measures. Ned Kelly was being considered as a full-time 'minder' for Cantona. That night at Selhurst, he was off duty in the crowd. From now on he might be assigned to sit near the dug-out at away matches. The *News of the World* reported that United players had agreed amongst themselves to report players who were 'winding up' Cantona to the referee.

The authorities made one swift move: Ken Ridden, the FA's director of referees, announced that from the beginning of the 1995–96 season, players sent off would be allowed time to leave the field in a direct line with the players' tunnel rather than being expected to walk round the perimeter. There would be other initiatives, according to David Davies. As well as the discussions with the Campaign for Racial Equality, there would also be a working party, involving the Premier League and the League Managers' Association, to discuss the situation.

Gordon Taylor, meanwhile, called on his members not to provoke Cantona on his return. 'Everyone should be given the opportunity to get on with their career once they have paid the price for having done something wrong,' he said. 'Everyone accepts Eric is a quality player. He was voted by our members as their player of the year in 1994 [amazingly, he was also on 1995's shortlist for the award, though Alan Shearer eventually won] and deserves a chance to redeem himself. I hope that all of our members appreciate the qualities they voted for and that when he returns there will be no unprofessional goading and intimidation. If we are expecting others to behave prior to the European Championships in England next summer, it is vital that there are no intimidatory tactics among fellow professionals.'

Sound enough, though it had been a while since Taylor played, most notably as a good left-winger for a then First Division Birmingham City, and perhaps he had forgotten the remarks made in the heat of the moment. One thought of Paul Gascoigne, once tightly marked by Vinny Jones to the extent that the Wimbledon player grabbed and tweaked Gazza's testicles. 'Stay there, fat boy. I'll be back,' Jones told him as he departed to take a throw-in. Intimidated and later tearful, Gascoigne barely made a contribution to the match. Later he sent a red rose to the Wimbledon dressing room; Wimbledon sent back a toilet brush.

The game has been cleaned up in many ways – for the better when it comes to tackling from behind and the professional foul – but there is a danger of it becoming too sanitized. Gascoigne, then a young player with Newcastle, clearly learned from the experience. It was part and parcel of the professional game and no doubt Newcastle dished it out too. The art was, and is, in learning to live with it and rise above it.

To call for special treatment for Cantona on the field – beyond the protection from referees he should be entitled to, and to which victims of his own tackles should also be entitled – was a bit much. The even-more gifted George Best had shown bravery in the face of some unspecial treatment during his days at Old Trafford. Special, though, it has to be said, is what Cantona is. And special is also how he thinks of himself.

9   Self Portrait

I! I called myself a magician, an angel, free from
                              all moral constraint!
Arthur Rimbaud, *A Season in Hell*

Footballers have always been regarded with awe, none more so
than Eric Cantona, with his physical presence and brooding
silence. For the modern player it is more complicated, however.
Into the equation of attitudes towards him in these high-profile,
high-pay days has come cynicism and disrespect. Players are, on
the field, what we want to be: healthy, heroic; existing as we
would like to exist: instinctively, spontaneously. It is so much
less morally painful to aspire to such states physically rather than
spiritually. They live those ninety minutes free from the mun-
danities of mortgages and money troubles, unencumbered by
office politics and fragile relationships. They embody our spirit,
and from the stands we bask in the reflected glory of triumphs,
share the grief of defeat. The result is often viewed out of all
proportion to its importance, but therein lies the passion of the
game and the sometimes misguided behaviour it provokes.

Off the pitch, the picture is less idealistic. The hunt for autographs and the voracity with which merchandise and magazines
are purchased can be at odds with the distaste of those who wonder
what all the fuss created by the game is about; those who believe

that players are overpaid simpletons with either hedonistic or banal lifestyles, lacking taste and social graces. The players are indulged for their celebrity by sycophants and hangers on but are divorced from the realities of life. Role models? You may want your son to don the red shirt and earn £15,000 a week doing something that stimulates him, but would you want him cast adrift in his mansion, unable to think for himself or relate to his fellow man?

It can be so, but it ain't necessarily so. A problem of football in the nineties has been the suspicion that has arrived with its new-found wealth. Footballers, more under the media spotlight than ever, know there is money to be made from simplistic soundbite interviews. Journalists are mistrusted, tarred with the same brush. English ones are apparently all desperate to find out the tittle-tattle and gossip, unlike the techno-journalists of Europe who are only interested in insight into the game.

My own experience, however, has been that once players relax with you – if you can get to them without crossing their agents' palms – and you have earned a modicum of respect, they are rather more thoughtful and revealing than you expect. Their range of views and interests is often rather broader than might be expected too. 'In principle, footballers are intelligent,' said Cantona in an interview with the French magazine *Globe Hebdo*. 'For they provide beauty. Perhaps others also read Rimbaud. I am the only one to have said it.' Then again, he told *World Soccer* magazine: 'It is fortunate that most players are not like me or there would be anarchy.'

With utterances such as these, Eric Cantona stepped into the melting pot of the English game in the winter of 1992, and the perception of the footballer–moron was challenged. Here was the footballer–philosopher with views on art, and his art. Some of it has been mischievous image-building, but at least here was a man who existed not apart from life but amid it, and was prepared to risk ridicule with his views – not in the least from fellow professionals who generally nickname graduate players 'Prof' or 'Bamber', after the former presenter of *University Challenge*.

Soon Cantona – unused to pay-for-say in France – also learned to get easy money for five-minute interviews which gave little insight. It was sad to those of us who wanted nothing more than to present an accurate portrait of a phenomenon, but Cantona's reluctance to speak in individual interviews other than those where he was in control was to some extent understandable with a tabloid press capable of misconstruing. In interviews on film, there is, contrary to the popular view of him, a shyness, which manifests itself as arrogance and stand-offishness.

Nevertheless, it is possible to gain a verbal self portrait of him from the times he has spoken out, in his own autobiography, in official videos and magazines and in the odd, less-guarded, newspaper interview, mostly in France. He might say that the following insights and views of himself and his beliefs should be approached in the spirit of Antoine de St-Exupéry, from his novel *Flight to Arras*: 'Pure logic is the ruin of the spirit.'

Cantona on Cantona

Extracts from responses to fans' questions in *United Stars* official magazine, January 1995:

I am a very intense person and so I am only interested in living life fast and hard.

I am always self critical but I know that the only way to acquire self confidence is to overcome the great obstacles of doubt and fear. Then you truly begin to exist as a human being.

I can only progress if I recognize my faults.

Success is something inbuilt. It is something which is a part of your character. I have a sense of personal pride which always drives me to win in the end.

I have never told a lie and I am always true to myself.

Am I cold and ruthless? Only to myself.

I have given my best. That's all anyone can ask for.

The more you know about yourself, the more you can set yourself free.

From *Globe Hebdo*, March 1993:

I have to be in harmony with myself to give of my best . . .
What is a functional person worth compared to an impassioned
one?

I am attracted by all that is spontaneous. I don't like those who
revise their work. If you correct it too much, it means you fear
the criticism of others. Spontaneity is my way of thinking; I
write only what comes into my head. Footballers are surrealists
because they create at the moment.

First I am a person, then I am a player.

I must give life to my gifts, otherwise they could turn against
me.

Why is there such interest in you? Perhaps I have something more
than the others. Among artists, there are those who risk
standing out and those who don't. To want to be recognized is
a side issue. As a child, I loved Cruyff and one evening I tore
up his picture before becoming myself. To succeed in football
is difficult, you must express your talent against opponents who
want to play better than you. More, you are playing in full view,
exposing yourself to spectators.

From *Cantona – My Story*, 1993:

He who has regrets cannot look himself in the mirror. If he lets
other people down, above all he knows he is letting himself down.

A young man has a right to rebel.

You need a particular talent only to want to please. I do not have
this talent.

You should listen and take the advice of others but always,
always, be yourself.

From *L'Équipe*, February 1993:

Does it not worry you, a Cantona at one with himself? No, I love
that. I play football for that. I live for that. But at the same
time, it can disturb me. In fact, I wonder if I really am good.
The more I read it, the less sure I am.

Do you never doubt yourself? Me? Never. But I am a dreamer, I
feel capable of anything. I see a bicycle and I am sure I could
beat the record for one hour, or win the Tour de France. You
should ask someone else, but I think they all think like me.

Cantona on Indiscipline

From *Eric the King* video, 1994:

I play with passion and fire. You have to accept that sometimes
this fire does harm. I know it does harm. I harm myself. I am
aware of it, I am aware of harming others. But I cannot be what
I am without those other sides of my character.

I don't have to justify myself. I have no regrets. I have to correct
these faults. But I must remain true to myself, that's the problem.
In the past I have tried to correct myself and I have lost my
game. What I have to do now is find a solution that works. I
think I have found one now. Nobody knows about it and I can't
explain it but people will have to notice it for themselves.

You have to do everything you can to ensure your body and
mind work in harmony. In my case, the wires often get crossed
so I have to find a way to achieve harmony. At a certain time I
underwent psychiatry. I didn't need it but it was interesting. I
suppose you could say everybody needs it. At any rate, it
wouldn't do any harm. It's something that interests me because
it deals with what you can't put your finger on. You can't see
it, you can only demonstrate it by seeking it out. It's like an
iceberg. The bit above the water is what everyone can see but
the really interesting part lurks below and that's where you
have to look.

From *United Stars* magazine, January 1995:

The thing I most dislike about myself? When the passion I have for football spills over and harms others.

From *L'Équipe* magazine, May 1994:

On the Swindon and Arsenal incidents: You have to understand English football. Things like that happen twelve times a week. Did you see the FA Cup semi-final replay when the Oldham No. 11 tackled Paul Ince? If I had done that I would have been suspended until 1998.

Without comparing myself to McEnroe, do you think he would have had the same shots, the same inspiration with the character of Borg? Impossible.

From *France Football*, August 1993:

I don't like to be liked or understood, just to be myself.

From *Globe Hebdo*, May 1994:

When I am accused of being disruptive, I reply that it is only seen that way because I am attached to an organized system. People forget that I have my reasons: I am trying to remain as instinctive as possible. Imagine dining with the woman of your life. She gets up to throw the serviette in your face, for a yes or for a no. If we accept that type of scene in life, in the cinema and the theatre, why can't we accept it on the football field? When I throw my shirt to the ground, or some other act of rebellion, it is because of passion for what I do.

From *United* magazine, March 1995:

You have to win, but you've also got to admit defeat so that football can keep its source of emotion.

Cantona on Life, Art and the Universe

From *Globe Hebdo*, May 1994:

What strikes you most about England? Unemployment, as in France. A head of a business won't dispense with machines because they come cheaper than people. And they don't go on strike. The more we make space for machines, the less room there is for people. I have my own idea for controlling robots: there should be a tax on machines more than on people. Then you could choose between the two. The money would be redirected to the unemployed.

I don't want to hear any more 'So and so only succeeded in sport because he is an idiot.' Not all engineers are intelligent . . . A mistrust of sport has led to a shame about manual labour. I prefer a good plumber to a bad doctor.

In relation to innovative artists, football is a minor art. In relation to creators of any sort, it is a major art.

What do you say to people who say that football is only 22 men kicking a ball about? They are without doubt the same people who say that money brings you happiness.

Do you believe in God? My religion is to give all that I have to give and then, if I have nothing left, it is not serious. I believe only in that which I can see, like St Thomas.

From *Eric the King* video, 1994:

I have always felt that someone was watching over me. I don't
know why. I don't know if it's real or just something I try to
convince myself of. The easier you believe it is, the easier it gets.
I try to convince myself it's easy. And when you are confident
you find freedom of expression. Freedom of expression brings
genius, brings euphoria, brings fire.

To achieve happiness you must sometimes go through the worst
depths of despair.

From *L'Équipe* magazine, May 1994:

In France, people forget that there is not only an intelligence of
the spirit but also an intelligence of the body. One does not work
without the other. Great writers have dreamt of playing sport.
Albert Camus dreamed of being a footballer. He understood that
sport inspires emotions that you cannot experience anywhere
else, even in writing a masterpiece. What can give you the same
joy as seeing a stadium and its occupants in such a state because
of you? What can give you that? Drugs? Perhaps, but sport is
healthier.

From *Cantona – My Story*, 1993:

I am not the first to have said that every artistic activity tends,
in one fashion or another, to embellish the world in which we
live. When you become attached to beauty at an early age, it is
very difficult to renounce it. A good footballer is by nature a
beautiful footballer and I already knew that perfection in this
area was a paradise very difficult to reach. In the history of our
game, only a few players have had the happiness to reach it:
Pelé, Maradona, Platini and Cruyff.

It is necessary for those in charge of football to understand that
there is no salvation without the artist.

An artist, in my eyes, is someone who can lighten up a dark room. I have never and will never find any difference between the pass from Pelé to Carlos Alberto in the final of the World Cup in 1970 in Mexico and the poetry of the young Rimbaud, who stretches 'cords from steeple to steeple and garlands from window to window'. There is in each of these human manifestations an expression of beauty which touches us and gives us a feeling of eternity.

Cantona on Football

From *L'Équipe*, 1991:

Today's football is of sweat and muscles, strained through effort. Me, I dream of lightness, harmony and pleasure. I am looking for a symphony but the football of today is nothing but hard rock.

From *Eric the King* video, 1994:

Football is my real passion. It's what I love most, it's what I value most. Football is the most beautiful of the arts because it is art. Art is about spontaneity. Every artist tries to find spontaneity in what they do. An actor tries to achieve the spontaneity of a child when delivering a line. A painter tries to convey spontaneity and freedom of movement. In literature I admire automatic writing. You must never go over things again. The quest for spontaneity is fundamental in art, and football expresses it best. Without spontaneity you can't succeed. This quest for spontaneity is beautiful. It's very beautiful if you score, for example. It's the essence of football, which is why I consider the game an art form.

Immediately after a match my frame of mind forces me to analyse things. Whatever happens, there are ways you could have done better. You score two goals and usually you feel you could have scored a third. That's perfectionism. It's what makes you progress in life. If you remember only what you do well and not what you do badly, you won't progress. You have to be aware of what you do well but try to correct what you do badly. Perfectionism is a need, it's not something you learn. Some people need it, some don't. It's a question of character, it's a question of personal pride.

Pressure isn't a problem. It's pressure that makes the game beautiful.

From *United* magazine, March 1995:

If I couldn't play football, I would burn myself out as quickly as possible. I have no time for longevity. Living fast and hard, that's what interests me.

From *Cantona – My Story*, 1993:

Money and cheats have trampled on it and they are still trampling on it. My dream has been shattered. I have been disappointed to discover that we players are only merchandise which passes from club to club. I have seen the deceit at work and I have seen the pills which you are advised to take in the dressing room in order to improve your performance. Yes, we are only expensive merchandise. Being conscious and aware of that will help you to take part more easily in negotiations with an employer because you understand how you are seen.

What I have seen in football circles in ten years of professional soccer entitles me to feel that our dream has flown away. But we must survive.

Where there is money, there are also cheats and they both go together. I would like it to be understood how many footballers do not play football just to make money . . . to cheat the spectators who have paid to see the game, to cheat the opponents, to cheat yourself – I find that impossible.

From *France Football*, August 1993:

A footballer earns the money he deserves. Singers, actors are also millionaires and they have the same public. Like singers and artists we sportsmen have the right to be respected, idolized.

What makes a footballer who lasts? Force of character. Spirit. A line of progression. To know how to give, to your team-mate so that he will do well. To know also how to receive from him. That he should know to give, to want to. To give everything for those at your side, you should want to do better.

Cantona on English Football and the English (there being a difference)

From *France Football*, August 1993:

I thought English football would suit me and help add that which I lacked. The search for effectiveness and realism. From that point of view I was not mistaken. I am a curious person and this helps me progress. In the end, that interests me more than my career.

From *Eric the King* video, 1994:

I like the English game because you have no time out from the match. For ninety minutes it is constant action from end to end. The English often say that the best form of defence is attack. They play to win. I like the non-stop action in England. You get right inside a game. Once the referee blows the final whistle you have really given it everything you have got. In France, on the other hand, the game tends to play in stages. We play, we have a big moment, we regroup. It's a bit like boxing. The guy attacks, gives it everything, then he withdraws. He sees how his opponent is going to box and he adapts his game. That's what French football is like. It's not a criticism of its effectiveness. It's a criticism of its lack of pleasure. There's less pleasure in playing like that.

From *United Stars* magazine, January 1995:

I think English football is played so fast it cannot become art. On the continent it is art because of the slower pace but it is not as exciting as the English game. That is what makes English football so beautiful.

I think the English have a more positive attitude. English football is about scoring more goals than your opponents. French football is about letting in fewer goals.

I love the speed of the game here. Playing from goal to goal, keeping the momentum going at all times. There's beauty in the game here because spontaneity is beautiful.

Everything is beautiful. The stadiums are beautiful. The atmosphere is beautiful. The cops on horseback are beautiful. The crowds respect you.

From *World Soccer*, July 1993:

They play too many games in England. There's the league, the FA Cup and the league Cup as well as European club matches and internationals. Look at the record of English clubs in European competition since they returned a few years ago. It's not very clever apart from winning the Cup-Winners' Cup, and everyone accepts that the Cup-Winners' Cup is the easiest to win of the three competitions. After playing in England I understand what has happened rather better than the English themselves. Before, English teams made up for their weakness in technique with physical and mental strength but now other nations have understood and caught up. The English believe they are the best in the world but the way things are going they must see this is no longer the case.

I like the English. On the continent we say that they are cold and reserved, but they are not. The English like to laugh. They like to tell jokes. I've been surprised.

From *L'Équipe* magazine, May 1994:

People say that the English are arrogant, but I wonder if they don't have good reason. They do everything better and you don't hear them speaking about it. We French always talk about it and believe we revolutionized the world with ideas which date back three centuries. In England, winning European Cups hasn't stopped them producing Shakespeare, the Rolling Stones and David Bowie.

The English will never change their game or their mentality. I adapted to them. After that, I just brought them a little fantasy from the continent. The niceties after the essential . . . You should not worship the Cantona of England but the England of Cantona.

From *Globe Hebdo*, May 1994:

Are the English more patriotic than the French? Yes, in football above all. In England, they prefer an Englishman to a foreigner. In France it's the opposite.

What is the biggest difference between the French and the English? In England they say: 'We have done it.' In France, it's more: 'We are going to do it.' The closer you go to the sun, the more rarely it is done. The North is more disciplined. The French give the impression of being artists, observers, originals. The English have their feet on the ground.

Has English football changed you? It has given me back my appetite for life, for playing. The English are not afraid to tell me they like me. If I am down, the goodwill of others helps to lift me. As soon as I open the dressing-room door, a bustle greets me. Around me I see only people happy in their own skin. That makes me feel better.

Why do the English value you more? Because the French took me for nothing more than a capricious child.

From *L'Équipe* magazine, May 1994:

In England I don't have friends. I know people, but I don't have friends.

From *Eric the King* video, 1994:

There are more teams with ball players these days and English teams do have a solid tactical culture. But they believe in their football, believe they are the best, although now they are noticing that there are others who can play the game. They love fantasy, but in small doses. They have players in this category – Hoddle, Waddle, Gascoigne – but they will always be the exception.

I love the spirit in the stadiums, like at Old Trafford, the special atmospheres in them, the great spirit that surrounds them. This is living football and the fans help you feel it. But I have my own way of operating. On the one hand I am very proud of playing for Manchester United. I have this feeling of enjoying something special that I might not find elsewhere, I want to win and contribute. But I must say again that I am on a journey.

The fans are wonderful. Everybody knows that. They know that, we know that and we feel it every game. We win with their help. The relationship I have with the fans is one of respect for them. When you see fans who have been waiting for you for an hour, who have been watching the training in the rain, then waiting while you have a shower, then you have to spend a quarter of an hour with them. It is an obligation. You don't weep. You have to do it because that's the way it has to be. It's not like that in France. The fans are not the same there. In France I have refused to sign autographs. There I have criticized the public – there's no love, no passion. People give nothing and only want to take.

From *United Stars* magazine, January 1995:

English fans are brilliant. In England, when you ask someone which club he supports, it means something. The guy supports a club for the whole of his life, whatever the ups and downs. In France there's no loyalty. If you're not top of the league, the fans go to another club.

From *France Football*, August 1993:

In England I have found a faithful passion. Not just passion when you win, but all the time. Faithfulness.

From *Cantona – My Story*, 1993:

I must say that since I have been in England I have never had any problems with referees. Firstly, they are the best because they are less theatrical and are not concerned about being the stars on the field. Secondly, they go about their job quietly and seriously. They referee honestly. You don't feel that they are corrupt, as is sometimes the case elsewhere. They make mistakes from time to time, but they are honest mistakes like we all make.

Cantona on Manchester United

From *World Soccer*, July 1993:

At Leeds I had become just another cog in the machine. And deep down I am not a cog, content to play a small part in a team who run on their own power. Why should I ever want to stay with one club for ten years – or even three years? No reason. What an awful thought. I want to maintain my spiritual freedom, so I was glad to change clubs. Manchester United play the football I understand. They are more constructive and creative.

From *L'Équipe*, February 1993:

Every time I join a new team, I am like a writer starting with a blank page.

How do you explain your huge popularity at Manchester United? I try to be 'exterior–interior' . . . It has taken me a long time to impose my concept of the modern footballer, but no coach has thought before to build a team around me. Manchester is a temporary haven. This transitory state is the future of my trade. The days are finished when a player stayed five or ten years with a club. These days it is ten matches, six months or a year.

At Leeds I learned realism. Or at least Wilkinson made me think about it for ten months. There was no place there for fantasy, and I don't think I could have played with Manchester United if I hadn't played with Leeds first. I also learned respect for tactics and discovered that I could play a game every three days without saying: 'I just can't go on any more.' In France, we make a big deal of it. Here nobody mentions it. It's not ideal, but it's normal.

From *Eric the King* video, 1994:

It is nice to play at a club where politics are kept to a minimum. Playing football is the priority at United.

On the death of Sir Matt Busby: I could not help sharing in the grief at the club during that time. Sir Matt made everyone at the club feel as though they were able to play with style and grace. Every player appreciates that.

Alex Ferguson is someone I can trust. From trust comes respect and loyalty, which are the feelings I have for Alex. These are great assets that cannot be won by chance. They must be earned.

When I feel I've passed my peak I will quit because it would be dishonest to continue.

And on the French National Team

From *L'Équipe*, May 1994:

I am not a Messiah. I am like everyone else, no more important than anyone else, but as important as everyone else.

And Finally . . .

From *Globe Hebdo*, March 1993:

I want to die from an overdose of love.

10   The Things They Say

Oh his breathing, the turn of his head when he runs:
Terrible speed of perfection in action and form.
Arthur Rimbaud, 'Genius'

The words of Erik Bielderman have often come back to me in
assessing the life – or should that be lives – and times of Eric
Cantona. 'With Eric you never know,' said the football writer
from *L'Équipe* who has known him all his career. It echoed what
Stéphane Paille, colleague in the '*Espoirs*', the French Under-21
team, and at Montpellier once said: 'Eric Cantona? It is simple.
You take all the articles written about him, all the criticisms lev-
elled at him, and you get a picture exactly the opposite of what
he is really like.'

That may have been just a flippant reply in response to a question that required more consideration than Paille had time for.
(What's Cantona really like? Well, have you got a few days?)
Bielderman, though, is willing and able to expand more thought-
fully. 'The way that he is looking at you, you never know when
you go to him if he is going to smile, to look past you, to kick you;
you never know. He can smell fear. When people are hesitating
with him, he can destroy them in two seconds, he just answers
you bullshit or he plays with you.'

Paille does have a point, however. Due to Cantona's mutability,

contradictions and unpredictability – off-the-field elements of his
personality that go into making him what he is on the field, he
would naturally say – he certainly defies typecasting, and almost
analysis. Almost, but not quite. All and sundry – the fat bloke
down the pub, as Harry Enfield might have put it – have had a
stab at divining what makes him tick. You can imagine Enfield's
Self-Righteous Brothers in the public bar: 'That Eric Cantona.
Lovely footballer. A veritable expert in the practice of propelling
a ball. But if he came round my house, kung-fu kicked my missus,
I'd say, "Eric. No. That is bang out of order."'

Some of those who have been close to him have been willing
to help arrive at a more complete and revealing analysis of both
the personality and the player and Bielderman is more forceful
than most. In his work for *L'Équipe*, he has followed Cantona's
career from its professional inception and become well-acquainted
with him: 'For some period friends, for some periods just a good
relationship; for some period cold, for some no relationship.' Isabelle Cantona even used to ring Bielderman to ask if he could get
pictures from his newspaper of Ayrton Senna for Raphaël. His is
a picture of a Cantona who has changed, grown more suspicious
of people, one soured by his experiences, who has become 'a little
big-headed' and is now 'a prisoner of his own image'.

Bielderman always found Cantona companionable until eighteen months into his United career. 'We have had a good social
time. He is a nice person, part of him. He could be like a sheep.
He could be shy. Then the wolf comes. He wants to keep this
image of a bad boy. He created his personality, he created his
talent, he created everything which helped to get him here. Now
he is in a jail, his own jail.'

Cantona's image in France is constantly fluctuating, according
to Bielderman. 'Most of the people are a little bit tired of him, I
think,' he says. 'Disappointed. They really believed that after two
and a half years with Manchester United of behaving very well,
of being with a big club, of enjoying the confidence of the manager
and the club, that everything was so positive he couldn't misbe-
have. When he was misbehaving on the pitch, we never took it
as something very important. Sometimes he was provoked by

guys; there was bad refereeing. This is part of Eric. Sometimes we saw on TV some image like when he was booked and sent off against Arsenal. It was because it was Cantona. He was too much under the eye. He deserved some yellow cards, sure, but not all. He walked on the Swindon player. But you have Vinny Jones. Just because it was Cantona it was much bigger headlines. He was not a very vicious player; if he was, he was a vicious player with talent. You have a lot of vicious players without talent. So we were bitterly disappointed and shocked when he was misbehaving at Selhurst Park.

'The attitude towards him is so-so. There has always been an argument between people. Who is Cantona? Is he Rimbaud or Rambo? Devil or angel? Cantona is both. People always change camps. It was fifty–fifty but not always the same fifty. I was against Cantona for years. I was a big opponent: talking and writing about him. Then when he showed what he can achieve, I was for Cantona. Now I am back anti-Cantona. The camps are always like that. If you find one person who doesn't change his mind about Cantona I would say he is a liar. You don't find one person from the beginning of his career until now that is always defending him.'

Gérard Houllier perhaps. The technical director of French football has remained a Cantona fan. 'I like him,' he told me when we met in Paris. 'To know Eric you have to know that he is an island of pride and generosity, and this combined, this pride and generosity, it's a very funny mixture because when he makes a mistake it would be very difficult for him to admit it, because he won't regret it. But what we say in French is that he assumes, you know. He takes the responsibility of what he does when he knows he has been wrong.

'He has a deep sense of justice. If he plays five-, six- or seven-a-side in training, and if you refuse a goal for any reason, and he's caught and thinks this is not justice, well, he can get really shirty. You've got to know him to cool him down, but you have got to know how to cool him down. If I whistle and say, "You're off-side," he would say, "Aah," then it's finished. But because he has got an acute sense of justice, when he feels that somebody is not just, or something is not fair, well, he sort of bottles it up inside and sometimes he can explode. When he explodes it is more violent than anybody, and you have to go along with it. He's so proud, and at the same time he wouldn't understand – just like a child. It's very difficult. Don't let me say that he's got a childish turn of mind. This is not the case but, just like an artist, he gets so furiously angry because something doesn't go the way he wants.'

Houllier, also instrumental in Cantona becoming the French national team captain by recommending as much to the French manager Aimé Jacquet, may have had his doubts at one point, however. After France's feeble showing at the 1992 European Championship finals in Sweden, Bielderman says he was lunching with Houllier. 'He told me he thought Cantona was a great player in a great team, but not a player who lifts the level of a team. And when the team is poor, he can be a poor player.' It echoed a comment once attributed to Michel Platini, who was supposed to have indicated that he thought Cantona was a big player in little games and a little player in big games; though he has since denied the comment. Platini has said, though, that Cantona seemed to want to score a goal only if it was a beautiful one.

When Bielderman was later in Leeds to see Cantona, he mentioned the Houllier comment to him. 'Eric suddenly went white. "What do you think about that?" I asked him. He said that he wouldn't play any more for the national team of France. I told him he was making trouble for himself, and just to relax, but he was boiling, he didn't change his mood. I told him I would go to my room and write the story, but to come to see me at four o'clock. I am not a tabloid, it would have been easy to make headlines, but I told him: "You will change your mind in two or three months." It happened at Nîmes. Anyway, we talked and I wrote a softer story.' Cantona did miss two games early in Houllier's stewardship, saying that he wanted to settle his family in England and concentrate on establishing himself with Leeds.

Houllier does not recall having said it. 'Anyway, it's not what I think now. He has won four titles: one with Marseille, one with Leeds and two with Manchester United. He won two Cup Finals. He had a period when he nearly decided he wouldn't go any

further with the Federation and the national team, and we played
without him in Brazil and Bulgaria, but at that time I think he
had probably had two months in Leeds. I think he thought there
was too much going on in England then. But I went to see him
and we had a good talk and he was very much involved. He was
a leading figure in the team.

'In fact, the opposite was right when you had a big match. I
hope next season will allow him to put the record straight in
Europe. This is a myth or a legend which is not true, because on
a European level he's not had much chance of playing, either
because of suspension or because the club was not involved in the
Champions' League. I mean, in international games he has played
good matches, scored many goals. Yes, he scored one goal every
match I had him, even Bulgaria, when we lost 2–1 to miss the
World Cup finals. He had a lot of pressure in that match but he
was one of the best to go with it. He's solid, he's mentally strong
– very, very strong. He's not afraid.'

Houllier also portrays a player, a captain, who is generous of
spirit to team-mates. 'He is somebody who inspires respect,' he
says. 'He has a very friendly attitude if you know him well. He
doesn't talk much but he is very friendly with the group. This
has been the case for all of the years. The group and the team-
mates like him very much, and particularly the young, the newcomers to the national team. He would put his arm round them
and say: "Don't be afraid. Play the way you like to play, and we'll
help you out." He was very much relied upon. He was a shield
for many problems.'

This is not, however, how Bielderman, as an outsider covering
the national team, sees things. 'Do they need him? No. Are they
happy without him? Yes. Most of the people around the French
team are anti-Cantona, including most of the players. But everybody was afraid of him: the coach, the team-mates. He was the
true boss, but misbehaving.'

It emerges, too, that Cantona can be something of an isolated
figure at club level. 'I think he's very much a loner,' says David
Meek, who finds him 'affable'. 'And while it wouldn't be true to
say that his team-mates shun him, or he shuns the company of

team-mates on anything important, I think on a day-to-day basis he keeps himself to himself. Somebody was telling me the other day that they had gone to the canteen and whereas all the players will instinctively gravitate to each other and sit next to each other, Eric will choose a quiet place and sit on his own.'

Chris Waddle at Marseille and Lee Chapman at Leeds remember something similar. 'He was quiet, yes, but I never had a problem with it. To me he was all right,' says Waddle. 'He's very focused,' says Chapman. 'I remember rooming with him, and he would go down to dinner and eat his dinner very quickly. He wouldn't hang around talking. Then he would go straight to his room after dinner. And when I'd come up at half past nine, the room would be in total darkness. I felt a bit uneasy about watching the television because it was so dark.' Social or withdrawn? Giving or taking? Probably both, as are most of us; certainly those of us, like Cantona, capable of severe fluctuations of mood.

People speak, though, of a generosity in him. Says David Meek: 'Most of the time he is so patient, particularly with the kids, signing autographs. He will go to more trouble to see that all the books of the youngsters waiting at The Cliff are signed. The other players tend to work out how they can dodge the waiting crowd: like getting a junior player or one of the stewards to bring a car up to the door so that they can get in and drive through the gap. OK, they'll pause and sign a few through the window, then say, "Sorry, I've got to go." Whereas Eric will walk out to the barrier and start at one end and just work his way to the other.' Chapman also recalls Cantona inviting him to his place in Provence one summer. 'When he socialized, he was a very generous person,' says Chapman, though he has had negligible contact with him since Cantona left Leeds.

'He has lost a lot of his friends,' says Bielderman. 'Lonely? No. He always has a new person under his charm. The day he will not be a footballer perhaps he will only have his family. He always has new people. All the people that have been friends with him will one day be disappointed.' Does Chapman, his first real companion in England, feel disappointed or used? 'In some ways. Eric sort of manipulates situations that will work for him, definitely.

I think most people who get on in life will do that anyway. I think he's very shrewd on the business side of it.'

Is Cantona genuine? All his utterances on poets, musicians, actors and painters suggest a literary, cultured man; an intellectual. One former colleague told me, though: 'I spoke to someone at Manchester United and they told me they have not heard him say one intelligent thing in two years.' Bielderman, too, has his doubts. 'In his book, Cantona says that he was born at the time when Gérard Philippe was capturing the hearts of the young girls in France but he was dead ten years before. Sometimes he will quote Jean-Luc Godard to you but you say, "This is François Truffaut, Eric." He wants to be intellectual but he gets mixed up.'

Chapman recalls something similar. 'This image he's got of being a great philosopher, he's allowed it to happen,' he says. 'But you can't knock him for that, he's making the most of what he's got. But when he mentions philosophy or talks about a movie where such and such happened, someone will have to say: "Eric, you've got the wrong film, you're quoting the wrong philosopher." I did to him sometimes. And you hear things like that, and you realize he's being very cute. He's played the game, which is great. Good luck to him.'

'Is he intelligent? Part of me would say yes, part of me would say no,' says Bielderman. 'When he talks, even if you don't agree with him, there is a structure, a capacity for observation. But sometimes he doesn't behave what he says. There is a con-tradiction between his capacity of thought and his capacity of action. So if intelligence is thought, then yes he is intelligent but if intelligence is what you achieve with what you get as experience, then he's not, because he doesn't take the lessons of his life.'

There is also a cuteness about Cantona, it seems, in his sparing use of English. 'I think he's very good at turning his knowledge of English off and on whenever he wants to,' says Chapman, who speaks some French. 'He wasn't stupid, that's for sure, but I don't think I really had the chance to speak properly with him because of the language barrier.'

'I think he understands more than he can speak,' says David Meek. 'Because even now, when he's trying, I think it's very halting and very slow when he's planning his words. He's an intelligent guy, obviously, but he hasn't picked up the language as quickly as you might have expected from a bright guy.'

As a player, few can disagree that Cantona has brought something special to the English game in general, and Manchester United in particular. 'He reminds me of Bobby Charlton,' says David Meek. 'Bobby moved so gracefully and was the nearest thing in football to a ballet dancer. I see that in Eric as well, which for a big man is incredible.' Where would he place him in United's history as a player and personality? 'Well, I place him second to George Best in both areas. That is a little unfair in the sense that his contribution in length of service comes nowhere near, say, Bobby Charlton's, and it's probably an injustice to some other long-serving stalwarts and great Manchester United players like Denis Law. But in terms of magic and skill, I place him second to George Best. And in terms of achievement, too, because without Eric I don't think they would have made this breakthrough for the Championship. I think he was the one who turned them from being a very good side which finished runners-up, into the team that won it. I find it very significant that without him they finished second twice and with him won it twice.'

'The best player I have ever had,' is Alex Ferguson's simple assessment. 'I have had some tremendous players but he has got things that win games, he has got things that influence games, and he has got the pride in his performance that inspires you as a manager.' The United players have also queued up to pay public tributes to him. 'He's got pace, he's got power, he's got balance. But I suppose his greatest asset is his vision,' says Steve Bruce. 'You always know,' adds Paul Ince, 'that if you are there, if you have got space, or if you are on your own, that Eric Cantona will pick you out.'

Ryan Giggs worships at the foot of the master. There was that time at Southampton when Cantona scored his chipped goal and Ferguson turned to Giggs on the bench and told him to note well the lessons of his guru. Giggs has since said that if he becomes half the player that is Eric Cantona, he will be well pleased. He went further in his own account of his career so far, *Ryan Giggs – My Story* (echoes there, too, of Cantona): 'To play with him is a dream. Eric is the extra dimension in our team. He is the best passer I have ever seen. He brings people into the game, up front, midfield, wherever he goes, he gives us so much variety. People try to put a block on him, but he's forever thinking of ways to evade his marker, creating space for himself.' Indeed, Jimmy Hill – by no means a prat, being often perceptive and always fair-minded – once pointed out on television that Cantona is adept at standing still, something that opposing players are loath to do, so that when defenders around him have moved on with the flow of the game, he is left free.

'When Eric gets the ball, he is brilliant at putting it out on the wing,' Giggs continued. 'He can judge how fast we can run – me, Lee Sharpe, Andrei Kanchelskis – and he puts balls out to us so perfectly weighted it means we don't even have to break stride. I think he knows how fast the full-back can run. And I've never known a player want to get involved like he does, demanding the ball all the time.' Indeed, he seized it when it came to taking the penalties in the Cup Final against Chelsea. Steve Bruce could not watch, but Giggs could. Erik Bielderman may say that 'with Eric you never know', but Giggs did that day, it seems: 'With Eric you know it will go in.'

'All that stuff about the ball responding to my touch like a woman to the caresses of a man she loves makes us laugh too but the thing about Eric is he works so hard to justify the poetry. When you see Eric Cantona staying on for extra training, brushing up on his skills, it makes you realize you can't be satisfied with what you're doing.' Giggs, something of a style guru himself for the younger generation, also admires the dress sense of his hero. 'Everything about Eric is cool. Unlike, say, Gary Pallister, he can wear anything and look the business. He came into training the other day in ripped jeans, a denim shirt, a denim jacket [appropriate for a man who had come to England, de Nîmes] and trainers and looked a different class. If anyone else had worn that they wouldn't have got away with it.' This is mostly true. Cantona can wear most things with conviction. But if his bearing demands respect, often his colour sense is open to question.

It was probably Mark Hughes who had most cause to be grateful for the presence of Cantona. Hughes had acquired something of a reputation of being a hard man to play with but the tag was to go away. Ferguson wrote in the foreword to Hughes's autobiography that the partnership was 'made in heaven'. He added that both had large egos that could have clashed but which, in fact, gelled.

When I met Hughes at The Cliff for the *Independent on Sunday* he told me: 'Before Eric, I did get a lot of criticism that no one could play with me, that I was difficult, that I was selfish, which I felt was unjustified. Immediately me and Eric hit it off, and I hadn't heard anything for two and a half years until Andy Cole came and after two games it started up again. It seemed to quieten down after we beat Ipswich 9–0. The thing that worked between me and Eric was that he liked to find the space behind the centre-halves and I worked between them for Eric to punch holes and pick people out.'

He amplified his thoughts in his book, thanking Cantona for changing his footballing life. 'His ability is obvious,' David Meek wrote on Hughes's behalf. 'He is a big man, but he has a touch which at times can be as light as a feather. It's his first touch which is so impressive; whether it is to kill the ball, play it first time, or hit quality passes with the inside of his foot. I must say, he has brought something special to the whole team, and I am not embarrassed to admit that we all try to copy him. He has opened new doors for us and he showed us that we needed to be more ambitious in our personal play. Now, thanks mainly to Eric's example, we actually try to outdo him, so much so that at one stage I think we worried Alex Ferguson. In one team talk he said [it may have been after the 3–3 'showboating' draw against Galatasaray]: "All these flicks and things, leave them to Eric because he can do them and you can't." We all burst out laughing, but he had a point.'

The French manager Aimé Jacquet sees Cantona's physical potential as his most important asset. 'He is a formidable athlete, capable of remarkable performance and he recovers quickly,' he once told *Le Sport* magazine. 'His movement is exceptional. In full flight, he is unstoppable. Any defender who wants to stop him legally has to have better technique than him. He has a real feeling for the game, always has his head up. Even before receiving the ball, it is like he has already photographed the play. You would not describe him as the orchestrator of a game so much as a trustee, one who holds the ball in trust for the others. He is decisive, instinctive, spontaneous and even confusing. Who could you compare him to? He is incomparable because he is so difficult to work out. Mentally, he is very strong. When he decides to be, he can be fabulous.'

When he decides to be . . . Jacquet is talking idealistically, of Cantona at his best. When ordinary, as happens to all, he can be anonymous, and there have been many reservations expressed. Even Michel Platini, one of his greatest admirers and supporters, said several years ago: 'Eric has two faults: he is sometimes too unselfish, and too often looks for the grand gesture. To become a really great player, he has to preserve his excellent movement but use more his physical qualities.' And Jacquet noted a few years ago: 'Sometimes he lacks the killer instinct in front of goal. There he is a poet, in love with the ball, seeking a gesture for its own sake. He does not use his powerful shot enough, perhaps because he has so many other weapons. Sometimes the game can seem too easy to him and there is a danger, as with all gifted players, that he becomes too static.' It may well be that they have since revised their misgivings, having seen Cantona's development with Manchester United. It certainly becomes clear why the hierarchy of French football saw England as a suitable vehicle for his qualities.

In England, probably the most damning criticism came in a brilliant interview by Joe Lovejoy for the *Independent* with George Graham, the then Arsenal manager, who ventured in an uncharacteristically candid moment: 'I still think Cantona will let you down at the very highest level. I think he let Leeds down against Rangers, twice; and in the big games, against Inter Milan or whoever, I think Cantona will go missing. He's a cry baby when the going gets tough.' (It was ironic that he should have plucked the name of Inter Milan from the air.) He is not alone. 'Well, in the end, that's what Howard Wilkinson believes as well,' Lee Chapman told me. The problem is that because of Cantona's ability, expectation is so high. It may well be, though, that he is not a player who gives a team its spirit, rather one who draws his spirit from it.

Cantona's detractors will also point to the evidence of France in Sweden in 1992, Leeds in Stuttgart, and Manchester United in Turkey. Devotees will counter with Houllier's evidence of him proving one of the strongest, and scoring, as France sadly crashed out of the World Cup at the hands of Bulgaria; of him winning big, tight – albeit domestic – games such as the last match before Selhurst Park, against Blackburn Rovers. It was also his late goal that had given United a draw in the home leg against Galatasaray and left them at least with a chance of progressing. And, as Giggs has said, his nerve held in the FA Cup Final against Chelsea. Even with Dennis Wise betting Cantona £100 that he would miss as he waited to take the first penalty kick. He paid up later.

One has to say that the jury is still out on the question of his performance on the biggest occasions. He has barely played in the Champions' League; has not done so in a World Cup. Perhaps Houllier's disputed words do hold a key, however, in that Cantona will enhance a good side but become frustrated in a mediocre one and, rather than bear the responsibility of improving it, will seek greener pastures. The best team in which he played before Manchester United was Marseille. They may have had as many top-class players as United but they were ones with egos to match Cantona's. United's players are no shrinking Viollets but have been well educated in the English tradition of the team ethic.

Houllier also cites another caveat about Cantona, though he felt it was one he could overcome. 'The best players are always characters all the time,' he says. 'But the characters, they make you win the match. They are those people who are decisive in the match. You can have eleven good players who say, "Yes, coach. No, coach. The grass is OK, coach," but it doesn't make the team win. The higher you go in talent, the more difficult you can get in terms of temper, in terms of character.' Then, significantly: 'You've got to be able to handle him in a different way because he can sap your energy.' You mean, he can take too much of your attention? 'Yes, you've got to be careful.' Like a gifted child in a family, he can divert you from the others? 'Exactly. Those talents, they always need to be indulged and the older he got the less attention you would need to give him because he would become more mature.' This appears not yet to have happened. It is only those managers, such as Ferguson, who believe in the importance of an individual within the team framework, who are willing to undergo the tribulations of such attention-seeking.

Houllier's first encounter with Cantona was when he took the Paris St Germain side he was then managing to Auxerre, who included the raw recruit. 'He was already a young, gifted player but nothing particular. I mean, we wouldn't exchange him, I think.' He came to change his opinion, believing that Cantona and Jean-Pierre Papin were the perfect combination for the national team: Papin the leader of the line, Cantona operating in the space behind.

It was the position that Ferguson arrived at for him. 'I think it is an ideal position to show off the best of his play,' says Houllier. 'From a tactical point of view, the way he helps position the side around the field is excellent. I think also the English game has helped him to make improvements with his technical and tactical skills, because in England it's not just sort of a heavy, close marking, man on man. So because Eric is very quick on his feet, good in the air, has good vision and sees things before other people, he can use all that when he has some free space. Then he urges everyone into good positions and gives good passes. To me, he is not really a play-maker. He is an attack-maker.' No Michel Platini, then? 'No. He makes the attack inside the opponents' defence, orchestrating the offensive moves. If you analyse the goals at Manchester, I don't know the percentage, maybe fifty per cent, maybe more, he's either involved in the first pass, the decisive pass or scoring the goal.'

There was a feeling, too, at Marseille that Cantona lacked a decisive change of pace to get away from a man-marker; that while he was fearsome once he had worked up a head of steam, if he could be nipped in the bud, nipped around the ankles, then he was a less effective player. I believe it was one consideration in his deliberations over moving to Internazionale. There he would be up against an entirely different defender, one with more intelligence and fewer scruples. I could see, in the more two-paced game in Italy – with the slow build-up and quick pounce – Cantona being frustrated and smothered. With so many other players of equal technical ability around him, unlike in England, he would not be the star he is here, would not stand out. If the eyes are drawn to him in the Premiership, in Serie A they dart like those of a child at a fairground.

'I think Eric did have trouble with man-marking in France,' says Chris Waddle. 'If you say he hasn't got pace, well, I don't know. But he has got good skill and he has got quick feet. And he's so strong he can ward people off. I just think when players are good with the ball and are confronted by players who aren't blessed with as much ability, well, he will find it hard coming to terms with that. Playing with Manchester United, he can do his work, never marked. Because teams here believed that if they marked Cantona, other individuals would do them damage. There is Giggs flying on the wing, Hughes was pulling you around. I think the whole Manchester United system has suited him down to the ground. He can stand there thinking, "Which player will I find this time?" There are times when it looks easy, though I know it's not. But I do think the best way to play him would be to man-mark him. Then you can get him frustrated. If you get him frustrated, anything's possible.' In that is another point about any kid-glove treatment of him. Frustrating an opponent is a legitimate tactic and one a great player has to expect.

'I think he certainly requires those around him to be playing well,' says David Meek. 'I don't think Eric is the sort of player who would carry a team on his shoulders, that's not his strength. And this is really why I would say this is the most successful period of his career, because he is playing for the right team at the right time.'

But man-marking? It is something that is always considered when a team is confronted by Cantona, and one can envisage, with a little relish, Blackburn Rovers crying havoc and letting loose the terrier with the bite of a Rottweiler, David Batty, to trail him for ninety minutes. The drawback is that if it fails, a team has lost one of its own players. 'I think everybody in the country knows that on his day he can hurt you,' said Waddle. He could say that again; certainly John Moncur and a few others would. 'He's got enough ability to do something you don't expect and I think that's what the fans in this country like. I think this country's allowed Eric to express his talent whereas in France, straight away, you know that you might be stifled. In this country it has never happened. They are better at man-marking than we are. There aren't that many here who can actually do it.'

Lee Chapman also believes that Cantona would find it difficult to slip into the role just behind a striker in Italy, where space is limited, with players defending deeper, allowing play to develop until the final third before attempting to win back possession. 'Yes, he wouldn't have the room,' he says. 'He likes to drop off into no man's land and get the ball, but I think he would find that very difficult to do in Italy the way they play. Here, the game is more spread out and you get that little hole that he likes to exploit. That's why he's so effective over here. That hole is his niche, he's found it and he's reluctant to leave it.'

In the tactical development of the game in England, such as it is, managers are now coming to deploy a holding midfield player, shielding the central defenders from a position just in front. It is something that Terry Venables has done with England, and several decent but not outstanding players, such as Barry Venison and Kevin Richardson, have proved effective in the role. It might catch on further in club football. 'I do think he's going to struggle now,' says Chapman. The question is, will defences be better prepared to deal with him when he returns? Richard Shaw, after all, had worked it out at Selhurst Park.

There is another reason why Cantona chose to remain in England: as well as being a diamond amid the coal face, he is, too, an outstanding figure off the field, which suits his personality and desire to be extraordinary. 'He's a very proud man and has a big ego,' says Chapman. 'He's definitely bigger here than he is in France. A lot of people are amazed how big he is in England,' says Waddle. 'I wouldn't say he's a big deal there. People have always said he's got talent, but when I go back to Marseille to see friends, they say: "What is all this interest in Cantona?" I tell them he's in the paper every day: Eric doing this, Eric doing that, Eric having a shave. I tell them he's very popular in England, for the press and the public, and the kids love him. And they say, "How? Why?"

'I have seen him more in this country than in France. I love watching him play, and I think he has deserved all his success on the field. I like Eric. He didn't turn his back on me at Marseille just because I was English. I found him a nice bloke.' 'A lot of it is myth and mystique,' says Chapman. 'I think the English are insular, the image of the foreigner has mystique to it and sets them apart from the rest of us. It probably could only happen in England. We are a breed apart, really, both in football and in life.'

He has put his finger on something. It could be precisely because Cantona does not give many interviews that his strong, silent, man-in-black persona is fuelled, the merchandise industry around him stoked. In some ways, it is a throwback to the fifties, when sports stars were seen but rarely heard. There was a novelty to them, a cult around them; a fascination with them. Their limited appearances – limited because of a less voluminous, pervasive and intrusive media – only heightened the interest.

In the spring of 1995, Cantona gave an interesting but sometimes dull interview to Sky Sports on Andy Gray's *Boot Room*, but discussed only the technical and tactical side of the game, before going to spend his summer in the Gers region of Southwest France, acting in a film as the sports-loving boyfriend of a girl whose father had quit the rat race and bought a duck farm. It was called, appropriately, *Le Bonheur est dans le Pré: Happiness is in the Field*. It added to the limited-appearance quotient and the element of mystery. Here was an antidote to all those footballers who will appear on satellite television at the ring of a telephone, or in the tabloid newspapers for the rustle of a note.

Perhaps that was why he is bigger in England, though there are other factors. First and foremost is the anti-hero so beloved of the us-against-the-world brigade and Nike advertising executives. With his frame, which is common in the domestic game, but with feet that are unusual in their deftness and subtlety, Cantona is able to illuminate greyness with fire in the same way those red shirts do on a dull winter's day at Old Trafford. Also, lest somehow we had forgotten, he just happened to aim his studs at the sternum of some scrotum of a character. And that, too, had set fire to the English game.

11   England Expectorates

All that I know most surely about morality
and obligations, I owe to football.
Albert Camus

A month into the start of the 1994–95 football season, *L'Équipe*
magazine sent a team of reporters and photographers across the
Channel. Something was stirring in the English game, they
believed. They interviewed players, managers, chairmen and fans,
to assemble a montage of the reluctant Europeans. The result was
a fifteen-page study entitled: 'The Revolution in English Football';
the conclusion: 'Foreign players, hooliganism all but gone, huge
sums of money . . . football made in England is emerging from
the tunnel.'

In August, it did seem like it. A new season always brings a
sunny optimism, and the anticipation of this one had been heightened by the summer's feel-good World Cup. England had failed
to qualify but it was won by Brazil, everybody's second team.
From the extravaganza in the United States to these shores had
come a posse of players to add a flavour of the expensive and
exotic as accompaniment to the expected. Jürgen Klinsmann had
arrived at Tottenham, along with the Romanians Ilie Dumitrescu
and Gica Popescu, whose international colleague Dan Petrescu
had joined Sheffield Wednesday. The Nigerian Daniel Amokachi had

signed for Everton; the towering Belgian centre-back Philippe Albert for Newcastle. Nottingham Forest had somehow attracted the exciting Dutchman Bryan Roy. Arsenal had Stefan Schwarz, a functional Swede with the odd trick. The dashing Eric Cantona, if still one of the few draughts of the warm South, was no longer ploughing a lonely furrow amid the two-a-krone Scandinavians.

There were, too, more indications that the Premiership was no longer just a bump-and-grind through a bleak English winter. After Liverpool's dominating passing game of the eighties, Arsenal's success with the power game in the early nineties, Manchester United, Cantona at the centre, had established a style of penetration with pace to which others aspired. Suddenly Nottingham Forest were playing with vim, Tottenham Hotspur, under Ossie Ardiles, with vigour and, above all, Newcastle United with verve. Kevin Keegan's new team was finally doing justice to the support of Tyneside. Seeing Andy Cole drive in a marvellous half-volley against Chelsea to start the ball rolling in a 4–2 win at St James' Park on a gorgeous late summer's day made everything in the football world look well.

About the worst anyone could think of was that new instructions to referees to clamp down on the tackle from behind and flourish the yellow card more readily, might emasculate the English game. Amid the whingeing, it actually seemed, rather, to be improving it. No longer could defenders just crash through attackers, and with the offside law having changed so as not to penalize a player level, teams could not just rely on a linesman's flag – even if some officials failed to catch the mood.

All this was being conducted against the backdrop of modernized, refurbished all-seater stadiums. The Bradford fire disaster, in which 55 people perished, and the Heysel disaster of 1985, when 39 Juventus fans died as the result of a charge by a band of Liverpool supporters at the European Cup Final in Brussels, had begun a change in attitude; sadly through tragedy. Football had become sick of such sickness. When 96 Liverpool fans were crushed to death at Hillsborough during the FA Cup semi-final against Nottingham Forest in 1989, it was the rock bottom. Lord Justice Taylor was called in to put football's house in order and his report changed the game. The new all-seater stadiums, one of a number of measures he recommended, were now finally built thanks to funds from the Football Grounds Improvement Trust, themselves funded by a Conservative Government willing to modify the tax on the football pools so that more money could be diverted to the game itself.

There was, too, the £304 million five-year TV deal with the BSkyB satellite station to televise the Premiership. These were boom times. It was about the only thing that Robert Maxwell, one-time owner of Oxford United, Derby County and the *Daily Mirror*, and the scourge of pensioners – and, who, incidentally, once tried to buy Manchester United – had got right about the game before going for a swim. Football had seriously undervalued itself with regard to payment from television.

Now it was no longer unfashionable to follow football, no longer a source of shame. Even the Prime Minister, John Major, could admit to being a Chelsea fan. Other MPs came out of the closet, having been conspicuous by their silence a decade earlier when Margaret Thatcher, looking for a new cause, had seized on soccer as ripe for a law-and-order initiative after seeing TV pictures of hooliganism at a Luton v Millwall FA Cup tie. Paul Gascoigne's tears, as England reached the semi-finals of the 1990 World Cup in Italy, had begun a process of football rediscovering its joy, letting go of its guilt. A glitzy new audience clambered to board the new rock and roll train. The fanzine movement showed that supporters now wanted to reclaim the game, and more magazines sprang up. BBC2 devoted a theme night to football and literary figures rediscovered its passions. The 1994–95 season, the Premier League settling into its prosperous third season, seemed the fruition of it all. And Manchester United were in the vanguard, the very model of a modern football club; the brand leaders. Cantona seemed the symbol of it all, a man who linked the mind and body, and appealed to everyone.

Much of the merchandising boom is due to United. A decade earlier, American football had enjoyed a spell of popularity in Great Britain. A lot of it was due not so much to the intricacies and excitement of the game, but to the street-cred fashions and

Americana that were its by-product. Baseball caps, shiny jackets and replica shirts all caught on. Suddenly, football clubs who were being forced to look beyond gate receipts for revenue, began hiring commercial managers and sending them to the United States to see how it should be done. Bobble hats and scarves would no longer do.

The main market was for the replica shirt. We could be heroes, just for one day, as Cantona might point out. Strips that had not changed for years were changed every two: amended, modified, jazzed-up; just to be different. They became street wear. There was the second strip, then the third, each rotating on the two-year cycle. Only United could sustain a fourth. Their lightish blue – their second choice – was the best-seller for two years. The first-choice red could never change – though 'never say never' the commercial men might warn – but then came a yellow and green halved shirt that was supposed to echo their early days as Newton Heath. Also a blue and white striped effort that looked more Sheffield Wednesday and bore little relation to their roots. And, of course, the black. The colour of cool. From the red to the black in one easy clearance. (The suggestion, post-Selhurst Park, of all white with a black belt had not been taken up.)

The arguments were ranged against them: parents being badgered by children for new strips; commercialism overtaking sport. On Channel 4, the writer Hunter Davies bemoaned United's greed in the *Without Walls* programme, *J'Accuse*. It recalled Keith Burkinshaw's comment as he left his job as manager of Tottenham Hotspur who had disastrously diversified into ventures outside their core business of football: 'There used to be a football club in there.'

United's response was that they were satisfying a demand. The best-selling shirts were adults' extra large, not children's. Besides, weren't football clubs constantly being told that they had to behave more like businesses ready for the twenty-first century? If they were to attract and pay players like Cantona, they had to raise the money to do so. And many United fans were willing to pay, pleased with the variety. As the United fanzine *Red Issue* put it: 'In the end, what we care about is what happens there [on the field]. Of course we all whinge and moan about the commercialization. But if a kid buying a United shirt in Portsmouth means the club has enough money to buy a Roy Keane or two, and it keeps admission prices down, then who are we to worry? Anyway, you've got to admit they've got their act together to make the most of their success. I mean, Liverpool didn't. They could have been making millions in the eighties. One good thing about greed: it certainly helps you get your act together.'

And there was more. Beyond replica shirts came mugs, keyrings, fictitious passes for the dressing room, 3–D posters, wallets, toddlers' romper suits and even duvet covers bearing the face of your favourite player, against whom you could curl up. Fantasy football. Books and videos came next, with United exerting a strict control over things in their name, though this too has annoyed some supporters tired of the bland, glossy propaganda they have been fed. In all, United now had 1500 items of merchandise in their catalogue. They outgrew their superstore on Old Trafford's forecourt, where it could take an hour to get in and get served on a match day, and opened 57,000 square-feet of megastore round the back, just in time for Christmas 1994. Shopping trolleys are provided. More shops have been opened in Belfast, Dublin, Plymouth and Manchester. Two others are planned for Sydney and Tokyo.

Match day is market day at Old Trafford. People arrive from all over the world. Accents and languages are manifold: personification of United's astonishing worldwide appeal since Munich. The visitors take in the atmosphere and take out their wallets. United estimate that each spectator spends an average of £2 on official merchandise, a figure they would like to increase by driving out the unofficial vendors down Sir Matt Busby Way. It is little wonder that the club have been so keen to invest £28 million in a new stand to increase capacity from 44,000 to 55,000. It would be worth the temporary loss of revenue (a reduced capacity of 30,000) while building work went on for the long-term gains both in gate and till receipts.

In addition, the official Manchester United magazine sells more than 100,000 copies an issue. More than 10 per cent of the Great Universal Stores mail-order business involves United merchandise. Since the successful public flotation of the club, Manchester United plc's own balance sheet has shown profits going beyond the £10 million pound mark, and that 30 per cent of turnover was merchandise. The impact of football on people's lives may be overblown and the figures of your average Tesco superstore on the edge of town may be higher but for the game, United represent a huge business advance in what was previously a collection of cottage industries. 'If we were asked to recommend the shares of a football club,' said a City analyst when United's interim results were published in April 1994, 'these are the only ones we would feel comfortable about.'

Even when there is not a match on, Old Trafford still attracts onlookers with their money. You can take a stadium tour for £4.95 (£2.95 children) and last year more than 100,000 did. Or you can stroll through the United museum. There is just a chance, too, that Eric might be picking up his mail from the front office; about three times as much as the other players. It helps enormously, of course, that United have a charismatic, photogenic group of young men on the books. Ryan Giggs and Lee Sharpe are cool and sell well; Peter Schmeichel has a cult following. The emperor of chic, though, is Eric Cantona. He outsells them all. Much of the new glamorizing of football has thus to do with United. In every street, in every town in the country, someone is a United supporter, will buy the shirt, glance through the glossies and view the videos.

With the unfurling of the European season the clocks went back, and so too did English football. Domestically Blackburn Rovers, solidity amid the style, were looking their more ominous, powerful selves, yet the multi-million-pound symbol of the new money stumbled out of European competition at the hands of the Swedish part-timers Trelleborg. Newcastle were dancing past Royal Antwerp of Belgium right royally, 10–2 on aggregate, but when their unbeaten start to the season was ended by Cantona et al at Old Trafford on the last Saturday of October, the darker days were on their way. United also began to struggle in Europe *sans* the suspended Cantona. English football was not as good as it thought it was.

November was a dark month for the game's image. The BBC's *Panorama*, used to looking into political and financial issues of world importance, turned its lens on the business dealings of the England coach Terry Venables. Ten managers were also sacked; the highest profile being Ossie Ardiles at Spurs, his bright side having leaked even more goals than they had scored, Mike Walker of Everton and Aston Villa's Ron Atkinson. This was the side-effect of the riches in the Premiership. So great were the rewards that relegation for big clubs was unthinkable, and this season four were going down. The panic had begun early. Also, off the field, the game did not appear as clean as it believed itself to be. 'Eric always claimed he wanted to be in a clean country,' Erik Bielderman told me. 'We have an image of English football where players behave, where there is not so much corruption, not so much black money.'

Around the same time the *Sun* trained a glaring eye on Bruce Grobbelaar. The following July he would be charged, along with Hans Segers and John Fashanu, of conspiring together and with others to give and corruptly to accept money as inducements to influence the outcome of matches.

The very fabric of the English game was challenged. Whatever else it wasn't, it was surely as honest as its season was long. The reaction was shock; at least the game showed that it was still unburdened by a world-weary acceptance of the possibility of corruption. The public appeared to feel a disbelieving grief rather than cynicism; any anger turning to sadness.

At the end of November the Arsenal striker Paul Merson announced to the world, via a *Daily Mirror* desperate for a scoop of their own, his addiction to gambling, alcohol and cocaine. Despite outraged calls for him to be strongly disciplined, the FA took the sensible, compassionate route and sanctioned a six-week stay at a Hampshire treatment centre. The reported £80,000 he was receiving from the *Mirror* would pay for that and at least some of his debts. Not far behind, his manager George Graham was exposed, in an excellent piece of journalism by Lawrence Lever and Simon Greenberg of the *Mail on Sunday*, as having received some £425,000 from a Norwegian players' agent, Rune Hauge, after the transfers of Pal Lydersen and John Jensen. Graham claimed it was an 'unsolicited gift', which probably made the Christmas tree at Graham's Hampstead residence a wonder to behold, but the explanation did not satisfy his Arsenal employers. An FA Premiership inquiry confirmed the facts in the *Mail on Sunday*, and in February he would be sacked by his club for conduct unbecoming. He set in motion a claim for unfair dismissal, then demanded, and got, a full FA inquiry. It confirmed that though he had paid the money back with interest to Arsenal – not Hauge – he had accepted the payment of an agent. He was banned worldwide for a year.

Just when you thought it could surely not get any worse . . . January made me shiver with every column I'd deliver. Clearly he did not know it, and clearly he could not be held responsible for what followed, but Eric Cantona's kick at Selhurst Park was to set in train a series of events that further undermined English football's new self-esteem. 'The way Eric behaved came at the worst moment for English football,' says Erik Bielderman. 'The week after came Chelsea–Millwall, you were back in the dirty years of your game. Eric was not the key point, but it came at the worst time and the FA should never have forgiven, given him hope of playing again. You are back in trouble. You have to show an example. Football doesn't want any kind of violence any more.'

The following Wednesday at Blackburn a spectator ran on to the pitch and attempted to reach the referee Roger Gifford, at the end of a match that had not gone the home side's way, and had to be restrained. The next Wednesday there was the near riot at Chelsea at the conclusion of an FA Cup tie that Millwall won on penalties. There had been an aura of hatred at the first match between the two, but the replay saw a pitch invasion by Chelsea fans seeking to get at the opposition's, repelled only by police horses. Chelsea had gone to extraordinary lengths to limit the damage, paying £40,000 for the presence of 300 police inside Stamford Bridge, five times the usual presence, and they would later be exonerated by the FA. It was barely comparable to some of the scenes during the seventies, but a worrying sign, nevertheless, that hooliganism had not gone away, had merely been contained. The subject of erecting fences again was even brought up, but memories of Hillsborough were too powerful. None thought that they would be, post-Cantona, to protect the fans from the players.

At the Manchester derby at Maine Road there were also outbreaks of sporadic fighting, with United fans leaping to cheer their team's three goals – and singing 'Three–nil without Cantona' – from their seats sited amid the City faithful. It was unusual in this day and age, and all the more disturbing for that.

The advent of closed–circuit television had done much to eradicate violence inside stadiums, with offenders easily picked out and prosecuted. But outside, in the streets surrounding grounds, it had never really gone away. Those who wanted the tribal thrills of violence could always find it. I remember in April seeing a leaflet in the road near the City Ground, after a Nottingham Forest match, announcing that West Ham's Inter City firm were in town.

Worse, much worse, was to follow one Wednesday later, when England's notorious travelling support followed the national team to a match in the Republic of Ireland.

Dublin in the rare old times was a delight. I had covered the Republic through the management of Jack Charlton and saw their rise as a power in World football – travelling to the European Championship finals in Germany in 1988 and the World Cup in Italy in 1990 with the team and their wonderful supporters, colourful and endlessly good-natured. For an Englishman it was a great refreshment after the excesses of my countrymen at major tournaments. The only drawback was the Republic's primitive playing style.

Match days in Dublin usually meant a bit of shopping around St Stephen's Green, a stroll up O'Connell Street, followed by a lazy lunch before Lansdowne Road. The stadium for a long while had no floodlights – 'They've no need, sir, they play all their games in the afternoon,' a taxi driver once told us – but now the ground was lit up for the visit of England. A foray into the city centre held no appeal that day, however. Reports were reaching us of trouble brewing. A few representatives of the old enemies Leeds and Manchester United had exchanged pleasantries at Ringway airport; Shrewsbury, Rotherham and Scunthorpe fans (for heaven's sake) had been fighting in Dublin city centre; passengers on Dublin commuter trains were being treated to beery Irish 'jokes' on the journey in from Dun Laoghaire, where many English fans were being ferried.

At Jury's Hotel near the stadium, as I left to go to the ground, a beer-bellied Cockney was imposing himself on a patient line of Irish men, women and children seeking entry to the bars. It gave a lie to the adage that the English are the world's best at queuing. It was as nothing, however, to what happened a couple of hours later.

Five minutes after Ray Houghton's goal had given the Republic the lead, missiles began to rain down on the pitch from the upper tier of a stand where England supporters were housed. Wooden seats were ripped up and shards dangerously hurled. The match finally had to be abandoned amid frightening, ugly scenes. English football was in the gutter anew, three Wednesdays on from Eric Cantona's kick. It seemed symbolic that the icon of yob culture, Vinny Jones, would later bite the nose of an English journalist in Jury's Hotel in a bout of supposed high spirits.

When I arrived home that night, after a sombre flight back to Luton with the England party, my son's first school essay was on the table. 'My dad writes about football,' it began proudly. Actually, I thought as I read it, he doesn't any more. Amid Cantona and the rest of it, he had become war correspondent, business editor, crime reporter and sociologist. It reminded me of the journalist, a football and boxing writer, whose son had once written at school: 'My dad goes to football and fights.'

It also recalled a few weeks earlier, when a Chelsea fan had yelled at the press box, as police were preventing a riot behind him at the Millwall game, 'Report on the football.' We would have liked to, and indeed still loved to, but what kind of duty would we have been doing had we ignored the sickness within the game; what kind of service to it, in this mother of all seasons?

We never believed that hooliganism had gone away, just its fires doused within grounds and damage limited around them, but here we were disproved. Those of us who earned our living around the game had clearly become too tolerant, almost immune to some of its ugliness. The anger and bigotry that spewed forth from towering new stands were a reflection of a society ill at ease with itself: it was hard to avoid the feeling that these edifices stood like Shelley's Ozymandias: 'Look on my works, ye Mighty, and despair!'

Those of us who came of age on the terraces in the seventies were used to the rites of passage, of seeing 'bundles', battles for territory, of youths steaming in or running from trouble, of witnessing a fan being led away from the ground with a dart protruding from his nose. So grateful were we for the sophisticated policing that had been born of the dark days, and which now averted such outbreaks, that we had tolerated men behaving badly. As long as they didn't wreck the joint, and out of fear of reprisal, we let the violence of language, the alcohol-fuelled exhibitionism, the arrogance, wash over us.

Those who rarely attended football, which was now being projected as a family sport with spanking new facilities, could have been forgiven for thinking that the mood had changed, that the game was rid of its desperate image. Football was now supposed to be like a visit to the theatre or cinema: a safe, wholesome entertainment. But the game is not like that. It remains a tribal activity that inspires high passion – its spontaneity is unlike any theatrical experience where you might be aware of the ending – and which mobilizes the uglier elements of society. Football can be an uncomfortable experience, even if you've paid £30 for one of the best seats at a Premiership game.

Everyone has their own personal experiences. Anyone who has travelled on the District Line of the London Underground when Chelsea are at home, or gets an InterCity train when, say, Leeds United are on the move, knows the insidious threat of violence that football fans can bring with them. If you travel by car, you risk its windows being smashed and stereo seized, unless you pay up to a fiver for a secure car park. In October I saw Manchester

United fans in Barcelona's once chic, now tacky, Ramblas district shouting and swearing unpleasantly, insulting the locals. In April I witnessed Arsenal fans behaving similarly before the European Cup-Winners' Cup Final against Real Zaragoza in Paris. Sure, there had been rough justice meted out, to Chelsea fans in Bruges by Belgian police, and United's in Istanbul, with innocents being punished. But sadly, the mood was that they deserved whatever they got.

There remains a fund of goodwill towards the English, a legacy of their role in world affairs, and a belief in their innate decency. My own experience travelling with football fans has been that any person who behaves with dignity and civility is welcomed and greeted enthusiastically. But this goodwill is fast dwindling due to the image of the Englishman abroad, specifically his assumption that he remains a superpower in the world order but is angry at knowing deep down that this is not the case. Around Europe in '94–95, they too had a problem, as the stabbing to death of a Milan fan before a match in Genoa had shown. But the English have exported this problem, and remain the role models for the hooligans of the continent.

And when you sat next to an Arsenal fan bellowing obscenities at the 'Eyetie Dagoes' from Sampdoria, though children were nearby, you felt little sympathy for the fan in general. The feeling grew at the Third Division play-off at Wembley between Chesterfield and Bury when I heard a drunken Chesterfield fan, on espying a child wearing a Manchester United shirt, singing: 'Who's that team dead on the runway . . . ?' I felt compelled to intervene and ask him if that was what he thought a child should be learning. It was a tense moment, but he stopped. To your own shame, you began to tar fans with the same brush, to wonder if you were becoming a fuddy-duddy. But exposure to the Club 18–30 generation, cans of lager in hand, swearing and taunting, was no way to experience entertainment. 'It's not all sex, sex, sex, sex and sex' went their advertising slogan. No, in the winter there was some football thrown in as well.

Inside grounds there are chants we regulars barely notice but which might horrify a newcomer, especially one with a child.

Some are witty, like the one – obviously untrue – I heard Leeds United fans singing before a match against Arsenal:

> There's only one Carlton Palmer,
> And he smokes marijuana,
> We'll be walking along, taking a bung,
> In a Leeds United wonderland.

But others are more distasteful. One of the modern favourites is 'You're shit and you know you are', aimed at visiting fans. Not that offensive, it might seem, but when it was given legitimacy in a sketch by the comedians David Baddiel and Frank Skinner on BBC 2's *Fantasy Football League*, a programme spawned by the new culture, it becomes clear that the attempt to tap into football's blokeishness has the effect of making coarseness acceptable. Signs indicating masturbation remain common, along with one-fingered gestures. A woman spectator, meanwhile, can expect: 'Get your tits out for the lads.' The jeering of national anthems that precede international matches still shows no sign of abating either. With the summer of 1996's European Championship in mind, the England coach Terry Venables had deplored it at Wembley. There, the tannoy was turned up so loud that the disrespect could not be heard on radio and television. A problem of the Taylor Report is that the best seats guaranteed no protection. In the old days of terracing, you could move away from the bore or the bigot, but no longer. You are stuck with him now, having been assigned a place for the afternoon.

The biggest problem, and most intractable, remains racism. The old standard 'You black bastard' is its manifestation. There was a hideous example of it in February '94 when Paul Ince returned to his former club West Ham with Manchester United. While the fans' anger at his defection may have been understandable, the response – throwing bananas at him – was certainly not acceptable. For years BC (Before Cantona) black players had had to put up with such demonstrations and reacted largely with dignity and stoicism, which made Cantona's retaliation the more difficult to stomach. Perhaps there would have been sympathy had a black player reacted similarly to Cantona ten years earlier. Perhaps the game might even have made more progress. Anyway, was it really racist provocation? Had Cantona, been, say, bald, would Matthew Simmons have fastened on to that? I believe this was more an episode of personality rather than race. Cantona responded in the way he did because of who and what he is. Let us remember, too, that though he may not have been blameless, Simmons was the victim. Cantona was not striking a blow for United or for the forces of good, he was merely slapping down someone who had offended him.

This is the underlying atmosphere of football, for all its gloss of improved comfort and safety, with its family enclosures and fast-food points. During the 1994–95 season, the Premiership's sponsors Carling – and therein was another shot-in-the-foot for football's dubious ethics; taking money from alcohol companies – produced a report based on a questionnaire aimed at fans. Fifteen thousand responded. One aim of the sponsors, for future marketing purposes (a by-product, naturally), was to discover which beer they preferred. But the report did reveal some interesting statistics. By and large it produced a flattering portrait of a game moving into the twenty-first century, trumpeting that 37.5 per cent of fans attend as a mixed group of males and females, and that 23.4 per cent attended with children, etc. Thirty per cent, they also announced proudly, saw better safety and improved behaviour. Which meant that 70 per cent did not.

Was all this sickness in this mother of all football seasons – not the least remarkable event being that John Jensen scored a goal for Arsenal – just a series of unrelated, isolated incidents? The FA, inundated with issues and scandals, had considered them so; although the FA's director of public affairs, David Davies, was to say that: 'If there is a link, it is in the area of personal responsibility of people in the game, and those watching it.' The Chelsea player Dennis Wise damaging a taxi – but being cleared of assault on the driver – and Arsenal's Ray Parlour's assault on a cabbie during a post-season tour in Hong Kong confirmed it. But there was, too, the question of the pervasiveness of money. Top players were wealthier than ever. It was a game coming to confused, painful terms, like the society in which it operated, with an identity crisis: opulence on the one hand, poverty and envy on the other. 'These are the days of the open hand,' sang George Michael. This was the open hand and clenched fist.

By the close of the '94–95 season a great deal of money was in the Premiership; and there was going to be more. Admission prices announced in the summer of 1995 showed big increases: a seat in Coventry City's East Stand rose 63 per cent; in Queen's Park Rangers' South Africa Road Stand by 30 per cent. The cost of the Taylor Report had now been found but clubs felt they had to compensate for losing two home league games, with the Premiership going down to twenty clubs, in theory a benefit. But it became a worry that it would all simply be eaten up by transfer fees and wages. The Premier League considered siphoning money into a new national stadium, bearing half the cost of it with the rest coming from the Lottery-backed Millennium Fund, so that it could make profits in the future. The more enlightened clubs – Newcastle, Blackburn and Manchester United – began to see that if the spiral was not to continue, damagingly, they should invest in new training centres and centres of excellence, where they could develop further their own talent.

After the Cantona affair and Dublin the FA toughened its stance, which was not difficult. After their summer meeting in 1995 they would vote Graham Kelly further powers to act more swiftly on disciplinary matters. The anti-racist message would be stepped up. There would be initiatives worked out with the Campaign for Racial Equality; meetings with the police to see whether the more relaxed atmosphere of stewarding should be strengthened; with supporters' organizations about the behaviour of their members. And with the Government to seek tougher penalties for offenders. We had heard that one before.

Cantona did his bit, appearing with Les Ferdinand in a Nike anti-racism television advertisement. The pair asked: 'What do you see?' 'A black man?' wondered Ferdinand. 'A Frenchman?' asked Cantona. 'Is it OK to shout racial abuse at me just because I am on a football pitch? Some people say we have to accept abuse as part of the game. Why?' Cantona did add: 'I know that violence is not acceptable in sport,' which seemed a little rich. Perhaps he really now did. The two, though, made a valid point. They should not have to tolerate racist abuse.

The irony of all this is that England is now well placed to host the 1996 European Championships, simply because its past well-organized police operations, refined to near perfection during the abundant opportunities of the last twenty years, may have contained and restrained the problem, but have not eradicated it. And the experience outside the stadiums of dealing with civil disturbances from Toxteth to Brixton, not to mention in every town centre on a Saturday night, reinforces this. Graham Kelly wants the Championships to be 'a celebration of the English way of life'. The hope is that it might be to the contrary.

The Premiership, named the greed-is-good League by the football writer Brian Glanville, has been another mirror image of English society's unease with itself. The smaller Football League clubs have been excused from the table and left to pick up the crumbs. Premiership salaries of up to £1 million a year, for Dennis Bergkamp after his move from Inter Milan to Arsenal, and transfer fees such as the £8.5 million which Liverpool paid Nottingham Forest for Stan Collymore, have served only to widen the divide.

Previous generations of supporters had a respect for sportsmen who were just like them but with a special talent. Now, many fans have only envy and resentment towards these highly paid superstars. In these times of high unemployment and low job prospects the less well off, the traditional audience, are finding themselves excluded. Some newspapers – possibly unwittingly, possibly not – fuelled the fervour by throwing money at interviewees for 'inside' stories, now that the tabloids could no longer compete with the immediacy of radio and satellite television which has pointed its cameras into every nook and cranny, and hyped up the game. The Premiership has loved its wall-to-wall coverage, but perhaps some of the novelty-value mystique is now evolving into scepticism.

These are lager-fortified, get-rich-quick National Lottery days, and a spontaneous and passionate sport provides an accessible, regular, and still-just-about-affordable venue and vehicle for the social resentment easily identifiable elsewhere in our lives: the angry and abusive drunk in the pub; the driver on the motorway coming at you with headlights on full beam. Football offers instant gratification for all these elements.

One of the silver linings of the Cantona affair was to focus attention beyond players' behaviour and their responsibilities on to that of fans, and it had been puzzling to hear little from them in the wake of Matthew Simmons, and again when a Sheffield United fan spat all over the Wolverhampton Wanderers manager Graham Taylor. After the Cantona court case, The National Federation of Football Supporters' Clubs did call for the likes of Simmons to be ejected and have their season tickets revoked, but Crystal Palace had done that anyway. I mentioned this to an official of the often outspoken Football Supporters' Association. 'You have to realize,' he told me, 'that a lot of the blokes we deal with are real nutters and they have my home phone number.' Sadly, you understood.

Of course, for their money – and increasingly more of it – fans are entitled to have their say, to scream and shout. It is a game that thrives on sound and fury, after all. English football's atmosphere, which produces such excitement, is the reason why many television viewers around the world prefer it to Italian or German football, both technically superior, but diluted as a spectacle by being played in the middle of running tracks. Also, football in Britain will always defy being fully gentrified; rightly so as the game of the people. With its rough edges that made it so attractive, it would never truly be the beautiful game in grey old England, even if its potential to be so on and off the field was evident in the US at the sunny World Cup of 1994. Without England, of course.

David Davies did have a point about personal responsibility. During the Cantona affair, my mind went back thirty years to a time when I was watching the non-League team it has been my lot to follow. By half-time they had accumulated a 3–0 lead and I made my way to the players' tunnel to question, rather too loudly, the quality of the visitors' defence. This ten-year-old boy received a punch in the stomach from the opposition's centre-half for his views. I have since acquired – apart from a distaste for Romford – a respect for performers and opposition, and was uplifted to encounter it at the USA World Cup. When I'm not required to be a neutral – though even then I expect the same respect I aim to accord to the participants – I believe my entrance money allows me to get close to the action without intruding on it and to voice opinions, if not personal, racist remarks. In return, I expect the same courtesy from the players for my role in the occasion.

Yes, of course, as Rick Parry, the chief executive of the Premier League insisted, football was changing and developing for the better in many areas, but 1994–95 had clearly demonstrated, Cantona at its heart, that there was no room for complacency. This damned exciting game is not necessarily damned. Just as Cantona is not an irredeemable character, so football is by no means an irredeemable game. It does need stricter policing, however. The Labour MP Kate Hoey, being touted as a future Sports Minister, has called for a public inquiry into its health, or lack of it, and unless the FA set up some sort of body with teeth, a compliance unit, to enforce standards and ethics, then it deserves one. The Premiership's new disciplinary procedure, rules and regulations will be watched with interest. If they prove powerless to prevent misdemeanours and worse, then it will be time to establish a coalition of the FA, Premier League, Football League, Professional Footballers' Association and League Managers' Association.

'Why do you still want to cover it, when it's in such a state?' someone asked me after Cantona and Dublin. Well, it's the game's very spontaneity, simplicity and intelligence. It is only when all the violence and sleaze is forgotten, as a referee blows a whistle and twenty-two men at the peak of their physical powers stretch sinew and lungs in search of glory, that everyday life and its problems are transcended. The experience and escape uplifts with a natural high; entertainment is a bonus. At its best, sometimes at its worst, football can celebrate the human spirit. It is when you see Eric Cantona driving or lobbing home a goal, or splitting a defence with a pass that only he in the stadium has seen, you are reminded of its noble potential.

Schools and parents clearly have the right messages to reinforce. And two of the sadnesses of the last season for me came not so much in Cantona. Firstly there was the report that one of the chief thugs in Dublin was a father of two. Then there was the schools match I was watching which went to penalties, whereupon the master took off his goalkeeper to replace him with the taller centre-forward. The team won but the poor, small goalkeeper was down-cast. What was the message to him – I don't really believe in you when it comes down to it?

Football, as well as a force for ill, can be a huge force for good and, as Camus said, a source of teaching about morality and obligations. It falls to the sport itself and those of us who love it to claim it as ours. The anti-racist, anti-violence, anti-drugs campaigns and the messages of sensible drinking and fair play do need to be stepped up. We must be brave enough inside grounds to speak up, with support from other decent spectators, when we encounter the ugliness. It falls, too, to Eric Cantona and other players to play their part – for the idealism of his views on the English spectator to become reality so that he and we can go forward in a spirit of mutual respect.

I took my son to his first match not so long ago, for safety reasons a semi-professional one where he could roam the terraces without fear. 'Look, Dad, a header,' he exclaimed as a centre-forward fluffed an easy, early chance. Any professional world-weariness I felt was banished in his delight. There are millions more like him, millions more than those who bellow obscenities at Eric Cantona, millions more than those throwing missiles in Dublin, who want to feel that way about football, about the skills of Cantona.

Or at least we must hope so.

12   The Changeling

We make up any excuse to preserve myths about
people we love but the reverse is also true; if we
dislike an individual we adamantly resist changing
our opinion, even when somebody offers proof of
his decency, because it's vital to have myths about
both the gods and devils in our lives.

Marlon Brando, *Songs My Mother Taught Me*

Finally, inevitably, in an interview with Alex Ferguson the subject
of Eric Cantona came up and the United manager mused on how
he might fare when he did return to action. 'Ach, he'll be all right.
Eric's a real professional.' I had been covering an Everton match
a few weeks earlier, and the taxi driver taking me from Lime
Street to Goodison Park was a Liverpool supporter. 'We'll be
giving Cantona all the verbals when he comes to Anfield,' he said.
'We're getting the leaflets printed with "motherfucker" on them
an' everything.' 'No?' said Ferguson when I told him of this, and
I expected to see the dark face that had become familiar to the
nation during the televised press conferences which punctuated
January, February and March. Then he laughed. It was a surprising reaction. 'Ach, I'm just no' go to worry about it any more
after everything we've been through.'

It was May and I had come to Old Trafford to speak to Ferguson for the *Independent on Sunday* in advance of that momentous week when they could have retained the Double they won with Cantona. Or lose both elements without him. It was a bank holiday Monday, yet here we were at 9 a.m. in one of Ferguson's various offices and lounges inside Old Trafford. This one was next to the dressing rooms at the old Stretford End. (His lounge for entertaining guests, which he does generously and with a bonhomie and warmth rarely on public view, I have been privileged to find out, is in the eves of the South Stand. On one occasion, hosting a small gathering of journalists, he was relaxed after United had beaten Galatasaray 4–0, and resigned to United's exit from the Champions' League. Subsequently he engaged in fascinating conversation about the old days of Scottish football, his own guru being Jock Stein, and – his particular interest being American politics – the assassination of JFK. He had visited the scene of the crime in Dallas the previous summer while at the World Cup.)

In May, however, the setting and his manner were more businesslike. Only Norman Davies, the kit man who had been escorting Cantona that night, was about, pottering. Even the superstore staff hadn't opened up yet, though it still looked a good day for business, with a few awed customers milling around, waiting for opening time. From a mobile stall the smell of stewed onions, which Lord Justice Taylor had mentioned in his report, already pervaded the air: the burgers ready for grilling. So, too, was Ferguson. I recalled the night of the Cantona episode, when unable to sleep, he rose to watch the video at 5.30 a.m., and ventured that he must be a glutton for work, a real early bird. 'Oh, I only need five hours' sleep,' he replied. 'Like Margaret Thatcher,' I said. 'Don't associate me with that woman,' he rasped. 'Somerset Maugham, maybe.'

To complete any picture of Eric Cantona, and the impact he has made on English football, it is necessary to attempt to understand Ferguson, the man who has drawn out more from him than any other manager previously. A fierce pride burns in Ferguson. It can be seen in his red-faced fury at times. Yet he is, too, a warm and expansive man. Indeed, a big man for a big job. The former United player Paddy Crerand once told how he arrived home one night in 1987, after a match early in Ferguson's tenure, to be greeted by his United-supporting son moaning about the team and how far, under the new manager, they were from winning the title. 'They should sack him,' said Crerand's son. 'I told him that Alex was a nice man,' said Crerand. 'I don't want a nice man,' came the reply. 'Just give me a bastard who's going to win the title.'

There is indeed a dash of the bastard in Ferguson to go with the Mr Nice Guy; there surely must be in anyone who succeeds at this level. To those who have crossed him, he can be angrily confrontational. At The Cliff, I have seen him banish a journalist who had offended him with some choice language, then move to another, shake his hand and ask him how he was. It may seem familiar, these two sides. Indeed, Ferguson is a kindred spirit of Cantona's. He was a tough centre-forward, for Glasgow Rangers, and had his own disciplinary problems. He understands the fire that burns inside Cantona. He had never the same subtlety, however. I suspect Cantona is the player he wishes he could have been.

Even this early in the morning with nothing more than a cup of tea inside him, Ferguson could be as passionate as at any time. The subject that was most concerning him was the attitude these days towards the sprawling success of Manchester United, and the way it had polarized in the wake of the Cantona affair: the bitterness towards superstore and superstar. 'The modern cynicism. People's envy of success,' he called it. Still, it was true that the goodwill and respect of the neutral had dissipated somewhat amid the moments of madness of the previous few months.

He had some grounds for castigating the media, 'who have been very unfair to us. But the longer you are here, the more you get immune to it,' he added. 'There's no point getting upset with them: it stops you doing your job. You just have to get on with it. But supporters get upset about what they read. They write to me saying, "What are you going to do about it?" Some of these people in the papers pontificate, when their own morals aren't so good.' It was not the media, though, doing the drop-kicking and stamping. Well, not in Guadeloupe at least.

The Cantona 'thing', as Ferguson described it, Paul Ince's

alleged part in its immediate aftermath – he was later cleared of
common assault at Croydon – and Roy Keane's semi-final stamp
were the main stains. 'One of my most trying seasons,' was Ferguson's assessment, which reminded you of John Major's view
of May's disastrous local election results as being a slap on the
wrist for the Conservatives.

Teams usually reflect their managers and Ferguson's response
to all the criticism was as vigorous as his charges' play. 'If you
look at all the things that have happened in the last year, not
one opposing player has been seriously injured playing against
Manchester United. There have been no gashes, no broken noses,
legs or jaws, no teeth out, no ligament damage.' You would
not, he insisted, see a United player's elbows rampant, which he
believed to be the curse of the modern game. 'No need for it.
They say you need leverage but that's rubbish.' It has to be said
that even Matthew Simmons had escaped serious injury.

The FA's ban on Cantona until the end of September still clearly
needled. The feeling at United in May was that, had they not
been pressured into making a hasty decision and so ready to
impose their own ban, he might have been available to start a
new season. 'The modern Manchester United player has to expect
different treatment from everyone else, from the opposition and
the FA,' he said. 'But for more than a year we have been playing
games like Cup ties every week. Every match is high profile, on
TV around the world, usually live. Players are asked to perform
at such a high level of intensity every week, there are bound to
be moments. We have tackles against us and we make tackles.'

From such statements stem the criticisms of Ferguson: that he
is a whinger with an absence of contrition and a reluctance to
apologize or admonish his players. But then, he was in a position
of being damned if he did and damned if he didn't. His character
was formed as a child growing up in the Glasgow district of
Govan, his fierce pride coming from a family who dealt with any
troubles, not in public, but 'indoors'. He also believed in treating
others as he would be treated himself. 'I had a rough time at this
club a few years ago,' he explained. 'But not once did the chairman
question me. Martin Edwards was marvellous. He stuck by me,

and so it's vital I stick by my players when they are criticized. I am the manager of the biggest club in the country, and when boys come here their families have a right to expect from me the best treatment for their sons. They don't want to go to their local shops and hear, "Oh, I see the manager says your son let Manchester United down." We know what we do. Nobody gets away with anything here.'

Indeed Ferguson has always insisted that any misdemeanours were punished severely under the club's internal disciplinary code. I wondered if there was a perception that Ferguson was soft with some players, Cantona especially. I asked David Meek what he thought. 'Yes. Soft with him and other players, yes. I think Alex is a very pragmatic manager, and his scale of punishment is governed by their ability. The junior players would probably have been out of the club. But I think he would be defensive about the major players.' Are they dealt with strictly, fines enforced? 'I don't know,' he replied. It does, anyway, seem an anomaly that any fines on players should go back to clubs, who thus stand to benefit from their own players' indiscipline. This is surely a case where money should go to a benevolent fund for former players in need, who did not make the sums of the modern player, via the Professional Footballers' Association.

'People talk of arrogance. That seems to be a common term they use about us,' Ferguson added during our interview. 'But where's the arrogance in Steve Bruce, Gary Pallister, Lee Sharpe, Mark Hughes, Ryan Giggs, Andrei Kanchelskis, Gary Neville or Nicky Butt? And no matter what you think about Roy Keane, he's a really down-to-earth boy. I know Cantona has an arrogance about him in the way he carries himself, but superior players can do that. You know, when we go to some of these places, they all want us to go up for presentations and they want balls, kit and programmes autographed. It's like a jumble sale in some of these dressing rooms. In some cases, there is an envy and hatred of us but they expect us to sign all these things.'

Is it not counterproductive to dwell on such perceptions and allow them to intrude? 'Aye. That's a problem, and it's something we have been wrestling with. We don't want to adopt a trench mentality. We just have to be big enough to take it. But I don't use it as motivation. The best motivation is a cause. When I was at Aberdeen, first it was beating the Old Firm of Celtic and Rangers, then it was the West of Scotland press.' It was not all whine and rosettes, however. 'Some managers have told me how strong they think I have been. And the people that have realism within themselves respect us. Managers, players, other supporters, parts of the media.'

He is, too, gratified by the development of a way of playing that's in keeping with the club's traditions, with wingers who take on full-backs and score goals, allied to midfield players of vision. There is such a thing as a Manchester United player, he agreed; the expectations at Old Trafford being different from other clubs. 'He has to want the ball, have the courage to want the ball. A player with imagination, a player who has the big picture. Cantona has got it.'

The other joy for him, he added, was his youth policy, which was now bearing fruit. Here Cantona is a role model (as a player) for the young ones. Indeed, in Paul Scholes, there is a hint of Cantona, with his liking to drop off a central striker and pick out angled passes into the penalty area. 'I also love coming in and hearing all the old stewards who have been here for years calling me "boss". I love to look out from my office at The Cliff over the training ground and see all the boys out there. That's what it's all about.'

During our interview Ferguson also let slip a sentence that did not seem especially significant at the time but now, with hindsight, may indicate the changing dynamic of Old Trafford in the wake of the Cantona 'thing'. 'The mood of one or two players changes, sadly, as well,' he said. 'They get a high profile . . .' He may have been referring to Paul Ince. Suddenly, when Inter came back for him after United's re-signing of Cantona, United were willing to let him go in a transfer worth some £7.8 million; the deal including two friendly matches between the clubs from which United would receive the gate receipts. Having spent so much on Andy Cole, United's transfer kitty was bare. The club insisted the deals were not connected, but there is, nevertheless, the £28 million for the new stand to consider, and they also want to finance a £5 million redevelopment of a site next to The Cliff to establish their own centre of excellence for young talent.

Ince was shocked that the club was prepared to sell him. He had felt that he was as important to United as Cantona, and therein may have been the problem. He may have aired his views too loudly within the club, indicating that he should get the same sort of deal as Cantona. That, it was pointed out, was available in Italy if he wanted it. Suddenly, too, Mark Hughes was allowed to go, to Chelsea for £1.5 million. It emerged that he had not, after all, signed the new contract that day at Old Trafford against Aston Villa, the fans having been misled. He was still concerned about pension arrangements and never got round to it. Then came Andrei Kanchelskis renewing his request for a transfer, its public airing annoying Ferguson who eventually agreed to let him go.

Fans were baffled by all this, then angered when it emerged that the down payment on Ince was to be only £3 million. Some discontent had been apparent in leaflets distributed by the Independent Manchester United Supporters' Association complaining about the rise in ticket prices. But the selling of Ince and Hughes cut to the heart of the club. Martin Edwards replied tersely that, of course, the fans were important but that he and Ferguson had to be allowed to manage the club in the way they saw fit. This upset the supporters further. Even the *Manchester Evening News* posed the question of whether Ferguson should go. In a poll, 53 per cent said he should, though it was a sample of fewer than a thousand fans.

It all demonstrated how things were changing at United. The plc were content to keep Cantona for the revenue he brought in – a new consideration, these days, and one that undoubtedly helped Arsenal in their decision to pay £11.5 million for Dennis Bergkamp from Inter in a package deal; £4 million of it going to Bergkamp in a four-year contract, and £4.75 million for David Platt – while Ferguson wanted to retain the different playing dimension. Without him, United were just another English club: a very good one, but not necessarily one capable of succeeding in Europe.

'I think Alex is Eric's biggest fan,' said David Meek. 'I don't think he has had the slightest regret about buying him. I would say that while he's regretted the things Eric has done, I'm sure he feels that the pluses far outweigh the minuses. He changed the rules really for Eric in terms of the code of conduct. Normally that's disaster, isn't it, for a player to be seen as the manager's pet, with a different set of rules? I mean that causes more dressing-room unrest than anything. But in the case of Eric, he's so good I think the players go along with it. I think the players would go along with him if they broke the pay structure for him. I don't think there would be any mutterings in the ranks about it.'

The pay structure may have changed. For a long while Ferguson had resisted doing just such, as had George Graham at Arsenal, ensuring that all were well paid but without huge differentials. But the changing English game now has to pay continental wages – and it now has the resources – to attract the best from overseas. Under their new manager Bruce Rioch Arsenal are reportedly paying Bergkamp more than £20,000 a week and Platt £15,000. There had been problems at Liverpool when John Barnes became their first £10,000-a-week player; with envy amongst other players, especially when Barnes was injured for so long and was not playing.

Was it possible that at United hints of jealousy were beginning to surface around Cantona? It was now rumoured that he had had his legal fees paid by the club while Ince had not; Hughes, annoyed at being left out of the starting line-up in the final league match against West Ham, also felt that he was left on his own by the club after his injury at Newcastle whereas Cantona would have been well taken care of. And Cantona was, after all, receiving a spanking new contract following the most serious case of indiscipline in the club's history. 'The most lucrative kick of his life', an article in the *Independent* magazine headlined it. He would not even be starting the next season. Yes, players put up with special treatment for special ones of their number while things go well, but should the success dry up . . . The *Daily Telegraph* even reported Alex Ferguson as seeking a comparable deal to Cantona's.

Clearly Ferguson would have to be careful about placing all his eggs in the one basket, making sure that he did not go overboard with the player he so admired. 'You should never fall in love with your players,' Graham Taylor had once said when manager of England. Then again, look how far it had got him.

David Meek certainly felt that United believed the risk to be worthwhile. 'There are one or two of the deeper-thinking fans who wonder whether United have invited problems which could deflect from their purpose. I think they worry to a certain extent that it's too distracting, but overall I think everybody, even those who see Cantona's re-signing as a gamble, think it's a gamble worth taking because of his positive points. I'd argue that United see it as a worthwhile gamble: because fifty per cent of the time they play on their own ground, where there won't be any visitors, so they are on to a winner with Eric – other than him getting into bother with an opponent winding him up. And I think half the places we go to have decent players who are not going to wind him up, and a crowd who are more interested in seeing him play football than trying to hassle him, so he's going to be OK. That just leaves twenty-five per cent of the time where there's a risk. And I think with a player of his genius, and a risk of three to one, it's no longer a gamble, it's an investment.'

Many have spoken of the game needing to change to accommodate Cantona, of other players and fans needing to be aware of their responsibilities. Gordon Taylor of the PFA had voiced many such concerns to me and a group of other journalists as we stood outside Sopwell House that day of the FA's disciplinary hearing. There remains the question of whether Cantona can, or should change, however. The assumption, on Cantona's part, was that he would not be the player he was should he do so. When asked once, if he would change anything, he replied: 'Nothing. Not a thing. It's not because I am happy with myself particularly, but I am what I am. I'm educated. I have my views on life, on my sport. Whatever people say about me, it won't make me change. I'll only change what I want.'

It was a question that Hugh McIlvanney addressed in the *Sunday Times*. 'It is hard to be confident that at his age [29] he can effect abrupt and basic changes in his complex, frequently explosive temperament. If he achieved such a transformation, it would represent a monumental feat of will and he would deserve to be welcomed back into English football with supportive warmth.' Meanwhile, he added, Cantona had to 'wrestle with the personal problem of preventing a long, enforced exile from the game that is central to his complicated and romantic sense of himself from becoming a spiralling descent into debilitating, souring frustration. He must struggle, instead, to turn it into a reshaping and rejuvenating experience, one that will enable him to return to action with his exceptional talent undiminished and his ability to control his destructive traits vastly improved. That is a tall order and nobody can be certain he will meet it.'

Erik Bielderman is sceptical. 'Can he change? He doesn't want to change. He doesn't even try. Eric will say he tries, but really he says, "You have to accept me the way I am. You must take the black and white parts of my personality." Counselling would be pointless. They should have banned him from English football. They create the opportunity for the next incident. If it is not October, it will be November – if not December, or January. It is not possible for him to stay.' Here are echoes of Jimmy Greaves, a man who had himself had the courage to change, in the *Sun*. 'I just think it is all going to end in tears,' he said.

Ferguson himself did not know if Cantona could or should change. 'Eric is an emotional man. We try to guide him and warn him but his emotions can't be controlled in certain situations,' he told Kate Battersby for the *Sunday Telegraph*. 'There's nothing wrong with losing your temper if it's for the right reasons. I can understand people losing it because I am that way myself. It's a game of great desires. Burning ambition can give you a bit of a temper. It's very difficult to change that in a player, because it would destroy most of what makes them winners. You're asking them to be something they're not. It can't be done.'

Perhaps there was a change beginning when Cantona appeared on *The Boot Room*, perhaps it was the beginning of a campaign to show the public that he was not such an ogre as painted. It had worked for Jürgen Klinsmann when he came to Tottenham. By skilful public relations, he shed his reputation as a 'diver' and became a well-liked public figure who would win the football writers' Player of the Year award.

And perhaps, too, something had changed in the relationship between manager and player at Old Trafford. One senses a hardening in the manager's attitude. He has indulged his star man, almost enabled him to behave as he did, with his desire to allow him to fulfil his talent. Now, having gone out on a limb for him, he could no longer afford to be let down. The very future of Manchester United depends on it, and the psyche of a team is threatened. Now it's time for a little tough love. Many times, it has been Cantona who has held the upper hand in relationships, been in control, like he so relishes. Managers have been frightened that he would simply walk out and the club's investment would be wasted. Any fear is probably now Cantona's: his next serious disciplinary offence is likely to be his last.

Ferguson may have been less afraid than most. 'I think if he is here today, tremendous. But if he is gone tomorrow, we just say, "Good luck, Eric, thanks for playing for us",' he once said. Cantona in turn had always spoken of 'just passing through'. But the parameters had changed. Where could he now walk out to? Inter Milan, perhaps, but the Italian transfer system allowed only for a window in November. Besides, United remained his spiritual home.

That much was seen in early August when Cantona suddenly asked for a transfer and took flight to France. He was, said the club's spokesman Ken Ramsden, apparently upset by the FA's decision to look into what they considered might be a breach of his ban: he had played in a training match for a United team behind closed doors, against Rochdale at The Cliff. He was being persecuted, the player felt. Alex Ferguson wondered if the ban extended to Cantona having a kickabout in his garden with his son.

Cantona was in transit when an FA announcement came through stating they would take no further action and that he would be free to play in similar matches. Ferguson swung into action. He had been in London, staying at the Savoy, to promote his new book detailing his account of the previous, traumatic, season. He decided to catch a plane to Paris. 'I suddenly thought: Sod it. I'm not letting him go without a fight,' he was later to say.

Ferguson phoned Jean-Jacques Bertrand, who agreed to arrange a meeting with Cantona in Paris, a half-way point, his client having gone on to the family home in Marseille. At 8 p.m. on Wednesday, August 9, Bertrand arrived at Ferguson's hotel, the *Georges V* near the Champs-Elysées, to take him to dinner at the restaurant *L'Ami Louis*. They would have the place to themselves, he told the United manager. The owner had agreed to open up just for them even though the place was closed due to staff holidays.

Cantona was already at the table when Ferguson and Bertrand arrived. When the manager saw Cantona smiling, he immediately felt he was in with a good chance of keeping his man. Over dinner – lemon sole the only choice, but the cellar's excellent white wines were available to them – Ferguson explained that the FA were challenging the club, not Cantona, and that it was all a storm in a teacup. He would, Ferguson felt sure, be given a fair shout by referees come October. Bertrand also felt that Cantona should stay. By the time the gathering broke up at around 1 a.m. Cantona had agreed to stay. Ferguson flew back to Manchester to announce the news the following morning; Cantona would be back at the club the following Monday.

Given Cantona's history, and the statement by Internazionale's owner Massimo Moratti that now was not the time but, yes, he was still interested in Cantona, United fans were hoping that Ferguson had not returned with a piece of white paper similar to that of Neville Chamberlain (not the former Port Vale forward) which promised peace in our time. Ferguson revealed that Cantona had even made a call to Inter after hearing of the FA's investigation.

The manager had read the situation correctly. The FA's action was minor stuff after what Cantona had been through in the spring. It was more probable that Cantona was feeling depressed at seeing his team-mates frolicking in the August sun and the likes of David Ginola and Dennis Bergkamp stealing his thunder. Life looked gloomy from his Manchester hotel room. He had enjoyed the summer, acting in his film, going on family holidays in the Caribbean and Cap Ferrat where he was amusingly photographed giving Raphaël his marching orders from the swimming pool. It was not that Cantona disliked English summers. 'They are fine,' he once told *L'Équipe* magazine. 'The problem is they last only three weeks. For eleven months a year it is grey – light- or dark-grey.' His daughter Josephine had also by now been born.

Cantona needed an arm round his shoulder; for the manager to tell him again how wonderful he still was and bring him back to the centre of attention he so craves. Cantona was also probably just as concerned as United fans by the departures of Mark Hughes, Paul Ince and Andrei Kanchelskis, especially that of his friend Ince who had so eased the pressure on him by winning the ball in midfield and supplying it to him in space for him to weave his magic. His career had shown, and the statements from witnesses confirmed, that he is a gilder of the lily, rather than the lily itself. Perhaps Ferguson, the most audacious of transfer dealers, as he showed in signing Cantona and Andy Cole, was able to reassure him. For the moment at least, he would give it another try, though the episode illustrated how fragile now was the bond between Cantona and English football.

Contradictions abound in Cantona: torn between what he says and what he does. He wants to be treated as just another player by the footballing authorities, and as an ordinary person by the courts, but as a special one by clubs. He is a spontaneous person, but has shown himself calculating when the occasion requires. This is the key to his personality and perhaps it can be his source of strength.

As a player he has the capacity to lift us above the ordinary, though without Ince, Hughes and Kanchelskis it will be interesting to see if he can assume more responsibility for the whole team, or whether this is a serious flaw in his whole make-up. But as a person, from all the conflicting testimony and behaviour, I can only conclude that on balance he is a good man, a good thing.

In his book *Strength to Love*, Martin Luther King referred to 'a tough mind and a tender heart', quoting Matthew 10:16 – 'Be ye therefore wise as serpents and harmless as doves.' He went on to write: 'A French philosopher said, "No man is strong unless he bears within his character antitheses strongly marked." The strong man holds in a living blend strongly marked opposites. Not ordinarily do men achieve this balance of opposites. The idealists are not usually realistic and the realists are not usually idealistic. The militant are not generally known to be passive, nor the passive to be militant. Seldom are the humble self-assertive, or the self-assertive humble. But life at its best is a creative synthesis of opposites in fruitful harmony. The philosopher Hegel said that truth is found neither in the thesis nor the antithesis but in an emergent synthesis which recognizes the two.'

Cantona has shown in his decision to face England again that he has courage, that he is a strong man. Now it is a question of courage in reconciling the marked contrasts of which he himself is aware, and rightly sees as necessary in any artist; in walking the walk along with talking the talk. As person and performer, he deserves his shot at redemption.

Index